Praise for *Back*

Back to Court is a must-read for anyone navigating the crucible of child custody litigation. In a process filled with chaos, doubt, and fear, Scott and Dennis deliver the expert guidance with clear, concise, and actionable advice needed to lead you out of the darkness and into the light. If you want to transform an otherwise destructive situation into a path forward for you and your family, *Back to Court* is the book for you.

Curtis W. Wallace, Esq.
Lawyer, The Law Office of Curtis W. Wallace, PC

Back to Court is a complete resource tool to prepare for the journey through the complicated court process for modifications and child custody litigation. This book provides terminology and strategy that educates litigants with all the major issues in modifications.

Brett Stalcup
Texas Trial Attorney, Law Offices of Brett Stalcup

In *Back to Court*, Scott Martindale and Dennis Brewer Jr. masterfully guide the reader through the labyrinth of child custody litigation with empathy, expertise, and invaluable insights. A beacon of hope and clarity, this book is an indispensable companion for anyone facing the daunting journey of a family law case.

Sydney Beckman
Professor of Law, Lincoln Memorial University

Back to Court is a vital resource for anyone navigating the tumultuous waters of child custody litigation. With Scott Martindale's unique blend of counseling and personal experience and Dennis Brewer's extensive legal expertise, this book demystifies the complex process of family law, providing clear insights and valuable guidance.

As pastors for more than 30 years, we understand the challenges families face during custody disputes. The journey is often fraught with anxiety and stress; it's a battle no parent wants to fight. This book doesn't promise to make the journey easy, but it does provide a compass through the complexities of family law, helping readers understand the process, the key terms, and how to make informed decisions. This book will equip you with the knowledge to navigate these situations, focusing on the children's best interests.

This book is essential for anyone facing or involved in child custody litigation. It's more than just a guide—it's a source of hope and empowerment in a process that can often feel overwhelming and isolating.

Ed and Lisa Young
Founding and Lead Pastors of Fellowship Church,
Dallas-Fort Worth, Texas
Authors of *The Creative Marriage*

Back to Court previews each turn in the winding road of litigation with clarity and compassion. As someone who has witnessed families going through this journey many times, I appreciate the authors' grasp of both legal logistics and emotional hurdles. This book will ease fears and equip parents to protect their children's best interests with wisdom and grace. It will be my top recommendation for parents headed to court.

Jimmy Evans
Founder and President, XO Marriage

Blending families is hard enough without adding legal challenges to the mix. With deep compassion born through experience and expertise, Scott Martindale and Dennis Brewer Jr. provide practical and spiritual guidance through every pain-filled twist and turn of the custody litigation maze. *Back to Court* is an invaluable resource, and I know it will bring clarity and hope to frightened families.

Dr. Jon Chasteen
Lead Pastor, Victory Church

I have been practicing family law for almost 30 years and *Back to Court: A Complete Guide to Child Custody Litigation* is without a doubt the very best book on family law litigation that I have ever seen. I intend to make it required reading for all of my new clients.

J. Neal Prevost
Divorce Attorney and Executive Director,
Center for Divorce Management

BACK TO COURT

A Complete Guide to Child Custody Litigation

Foreword by Jay Sekulow

BACK TO COURT

A Complete Guide to Child Custody Litigation

SCOTT MARTINDALE, LPC-S
& DENNIS BREWER JR, JD

with Vanessa Martindale, RN, BSN

Back to Court: A Complete Guide to Child Custody Litigation
Copyright © 2024 by Scott Martindale, LPC-S and Dennis Brewer Jr, JD

ISBN: 978–1–960870-20-9 Paperback
ISBN: 978–1–960870-21-6 eBook

XO Publishing is a leading creator of relationship-based resources. We focus primarily on marriage-related content for churches, small group curriculum, and people looking for timeless truths about relationships and overall marital health. For more information on other resources from XO Publishing, visit XOMarriage.com.

XO Marriage®, an imprint of XO Publishing
1021 Grace Lane
Southlake, Texas 76092

Printed in the United States of America
24 25 26 27—5 4 3 2 1

CONTENTS

DEDICATION

To the reader who never wanted to pick up this book, we see you. To the family that is struggling for an answer after being served court papers, we see you. To the mother, father, stepmom, or step-dad trying to navigate tomorrow's challenges of what's next, we see you. More importantly, our Father in heaven sees you.

If you're scared, there's hope. If you're angry, there's healing. If you're defeated, there's a promise of a better tomorrow. Please read this book with an open heart to learn, with an open mind to see what's unseen, and with faith in the promise that there will be purpose through your pain. Healing is possible through God's love, and our hope is that you will be filled with knowledge, understanding, and hope for a brighter and blessed future.

FOREWORD

As an attorney, I've dedicated my professional life to helping and protecting families. In my experience, legal clients are best served when they understand the process and have realistic expectations about potential outcomes. Litigation is nobody's favorite word. A legal battlefield is fraught with stress and anxiety, and it depletes emotional energy. No matter why you picked up this book, you will find hope for hurting families. You are not alone! This book provides tools to guide you through the challenging process and ensure the emotional and physical well-being of your children.

Licensed professional counselor Scott Martindale and attorney Dennis Brewer have collaborated from different areas of professional expertise to provide a valuable resource. They cover the full scope of blended family litigation: before, during, and after a custody modification lawsuit. To help you understand the process, the authors describe the big picture with clear explanations of legal terms and the court system. On the personal level, they talk straight about your responsibilities to review documentation and seek a realistic outcome. This resource prepares families for success through the rough road that can be terrifying. You can be prepared to go into the process knowing what is in store for you and your family. The goal of this book is to provide you with the tools to achieve a clear, workable plan that everyone can follow for the best interest of the children.

My hope is that after reading this book, readers will soak up the wisdom offered and be encouraged despite their current legal challenges. This is a must-read for plaintiffs and defendants alike who are navigating custody modifications. It's the kind of book that will inspire you to dream of a better future.

Jay Sekulow, JD, PhD
BA 1977
JD 1980 Mercer University
PhD 2004 Regent University
Author of *And Nothing But the Truth:*
Real Life Stories of Americans Defending Their Faith
and Protecting Their Families (1996)

PREFACE

Scott

My wife, Vanessa, and I wrote a book last year titled *Blended and Redeemed: The Go-To Field Guide for the Modern Stepfamily.* We spent one chapter of that book discussing litigation issues because we'd been through them ourselves. We also had talked to so many families who had either been through the process of blending or were headed into it. They had tons of questions, so we thought it would be worth dedicating a chapter to answering the most common questions. After the book came out, we were a little surprised when *that* chapter—"Litigation: Your New, Least-Favorite Hobby"—was the one that readers commented on the most. Whenever we spoke at a conference or led a workshop, several people would approach us and say some version of, "I read your book. The chapter on litigation was so helpful, but what about *(insert specific question here)*?" Our friends started joking that we should have written a whole book *just* about litigation. Eventually, we got the message.

After discussing it for several weeks, Vanessa and I decided this was an opportunity to create a valuable resource that covered the full scope of blended family litigation: before, during, and after a custody modification lawsuit. We were amazed at how few resources there were for families facing this tragic yet common reality. Every day we work with blended families through our Blended Kingdom Families ministry and our Texas-based counseling center, SEVN Therapy Co., so we know how critical the litigation issue is. There is a definite need for a manual on the ins and outs of family law litigation to prepare these moms, dads, and stepparents for the rough road ahead of them.

So we chose to do our best to provide some help for this special group of hurting families. Rather than co-authoring this book together, as we did for *Blended and Redeemed*, we decided the best thing to do was to invite our good friend Dennis Brewer Jr. to write this book with me. Dennis spent nearly 25 years in private practice as an attorney specializing in family law before accepting the call to executive ministry in a large church. With his family law and ministry background, I knew he'd be the perfect partner to come alongside me to bring this crucial information to the millions of families across the country who are struggling to navigate the mine field of family litigation. We pray that this book becomes a trusted and valuable resource to you and your family as you join the fray, whether you're the one filing the suit or the one who's been served papers. Speaking as one who's been through it, I can assure you there is hope, and you *will* get through these dark days. Dennis and I can help.

LEGALESE 101

A Glossary for Beginners

One of the most intimidating parts of litigation is the realization that everyone around you has suddenly started speaking in a different language. Words and phrases you've never heard before are thrown around loosely. People start nonchalantly dropping Latin terms into conversations like it's a perfectly normal thing for non-lawyers to do. (It's not.) If your attorney doesn't take the time and effort to do some foundational education—not to mention hand-holding—it's easy to feel lost, almost like you've been dropped into a foreign land without as much as a phrase book to help you get by. In those moments, all we need to feel some sense of security is a little context and a sliver of understanding to pierce the clouds of verbal chaos. That's what the next several pages are for.

Here, we want to help you prepare for the road ahead by defining some of the key terms, people, and positions that you are likely to encounter throughout your litigation experience. Think of this as your ready-reference phrase book for the wild and untamed foreign land of litigation. We're presenting this here as a layman's glossary to use for reference as needed, but we also encourage you to read through each term carefully now. We will use these terms throughout the rest of the book, and more importantly, the attorneys and other court officials involved in your case will use them throughout your litigation—usually without stopping to make sure you know what they're talking about. So you might as well learn them now.

Legal Terminology: Process

Attorney-Client Contract

Sets the terms of legal representation. Commonly in a letter format, although can be in a more formal instrument. Typically includes subject matter of representation; scope of the engagement; the attorney responsible for the case; fee structure, including recitation of hourly rates for those who might work on the case; payment terms, including retainer requirements and evergreen provisions; and a signature line for the client evidencing his/her acceptance and agreement to the terms.

Alternative Dispute Resolution (ADR) Procedures

Options for resolving disputes between parties outside the courtroom and as an alternative to a trial, such as *mediation* and *arbitration*, the latter of which can be binding or nonbinding. In the case of mediation, a neutral third party is used to facilitate the parties reaching an agreement. In the case of arbitration, a neutral third party or panel is used to make findings and/or a ruling in lieu of a judge or jury.

Appeal

A legal process for having a previous lower court (trial court) ruling or judgment reviewed and possibly overturned by an appellate court. This is typically handled by an appellate law specialist.

Appellate Courts

State and federal courts that hear appeals from *trial courts*. The issues are limited to matters of law, not facts. States can have multiple appellate courts dispersed geographically that have intermediate appellate jurisdiction to hear appeals from family law as well as other types of cases. States also can have a higher appellate court (supreme court) that is the state's appellate court of last resort that, if requested, may or may not review a case ruled on by an intermediate appellate court.

Arbitration
An *alternative dispute resolution* procedure in which an *arbitrator* or a panel of arbitrators rule on the issues. Rulings can be binding or nonbinding and can be faith-based. Typically, the rules of procedure and evidence are relaxed compared to a trial and the proceedings are not held in a forum like a courtroom, which is open to the public.

Bench Trial; Trial by Court (TBC)
All issues are presented to the presiding judge.

Best Interest of Child
The primary consideration of the court in determining the issues of conservatorship, possession of, and access to the child.

Billable Hours and Hourly Rate
Typically, attorneys in a family law case bill for their services and the services of their staff by the hour. The rate varies for partners, associate attorneys, paralegals, and other support staff.

Child Custody Case
A common term for a lawsuit that involves the issue of which party should be awarded primary custody or possession of the child(ren) and the right to establish the legal domicile of the child(ren).

Child Custody Evaluation
An evaluation process ordered by a court in a contested case. The evaluation process gathers information, opinions, recommendations, and answers to specific questions asked by the court regarding conservatorship of a child. This includes the terms and conditions of conservatorship; possession of or access to a child, including the terms and conditions of possession or access; or any other issue affecting the best interest of a child. The results of the evaluation are given to the court, the parties to the suit, the parties' attorneys, and any other person appointed by the court in the suit.

Child's Primary Residence

The child's principal dwelling place and typically where the child will live at least one-half or the majority of the time. Typically assigned to the residence of a *party* in the case or to a geographic area.

Collaborative Law

A newer form of *alternative dispute resolution* designed to resolve issues by agreement in a collaborative process without utilizing typical forms of discovery and court determinations and/or rulings. Typically, the process makes the use of agreed-upon experts as opposed to dueling experts retained by each side. Generally, if the parties are unsuccessful in resolving their issues when the collaborative process has been utilized and must turn to the court and a trial to resolve the issues, the collaborative lawyers must withdraw from the case.

Court of Continuing Jurisdiction

Generally, a *court of continuing jurisdiction* is a court that has the right to modify or enforce its previous rulings or orders. In Texas, for example, a court in a divorce action acquires continuing, exclusive jurisdiction over matters of the parent-child relationship upon the *rendition* (ruling) of a final order.

Depositions

The classic discovery tool. *Depositions*, or "depo" for short, is a procedure where the person being deposed is placed under oath (subject to the penalty of perjury) and questioned just as if they were in the courtroom testifying from the witness stand, except there is no judge present. There are different rules that govern the scope of inquiry and the objections that may be made during a deposition than those that govern the admissibility of evidence during a trial proceeding. Typically, a deposition is taken in one of the attorney's law offices; each party and their attorney has a right to be present and question the person being deposed. The scope of the questions is broader in a deposition than what is allowed at trial, where the requirement of relevancy governs. In a deposition, generally the limit on the questioning is whether the question is reasonably calculated to lead to the discovery of admissible evidence. Typically, a stenographer (private court reporter) takes down all questions, answers, and objections or comments made on the record. With notice, the deposition may be videorecorded. Either party to the suit can take a limited number of depositions or limited hours of depositions in a pending suit of opposing parties and nonparty witnesses. The deposition testimony may be read into evidence at trial and/or used to impeach the witness if their testimony is inconsistent.

Discovery
A term used to describe the various tools of gathering information from the opposing party or third parties (witnesses/non-parties) that are reasonably calculated to lead to the discovery of admissible evidence.

Docket
The term as used in family court proceedings typically refers to the court's calendar for trial settings. For example, a case is on the court's trial docket for a particular week/day/term that the court sets cases for trial. The case may be set alone or with a group of cases, and one, some, or all may be called to trial depending on the time available. If set in a group, the cases are assigned a position and are taken to trial in order.

Entry
The filing of a signed judgment or order of the court with the *clerk of the court*. The date of entry is considered the date the judgment becomes final for appellate purposes.

Family Violence Protective Order
A protective order with quasi-criminal ramifications for future violation, including arrest. The order may be granted when there is

sufficient evidence that family violence has occurred and is likely to occur in the future.

Geographic Restriction
Requires a child's residence to remain in a particular geographic area.

High-Conflict Case
Refers to a SAPCR case in which the parties have continually taken disputes to the adjudication process and/or is marked by anger, distrust, and inability to communicate about and cooperate in the care of their children.

Impeach
To challenge the credibility or truthfulness of sworn testimony of a witness or party with a prior inconsistent statement or other conflicting evidence.

Injunction
A civil court order that requires a person to do or refrain from doing something. There are generally three types of injunctions:

- *Temporary restraining order* (TRO), which is of short duration and may be granted *ex parte* (without the opposing party's participation).
- *Temporary injunction,* which is generally in effect during the pendency of a suit.
- *Permanent injunction,* which goes into effect after the suit has concluded.

TROs and temporary injunctions are very common in divorce suits and are designed to protect the parties and their assets.

Jurisdiction
The authority of a court to make decisions in a particular case.

Jury Trial; Trial by Jury (TBJ)

Some or all issues of fact are presented to a jury for determination. The availability of a jury trial in a family law case varies from jurisdiction to jurisdiction and typically, if available, must be timely requested.

Material and Substantial Change of Circumstances

One of the two primary grounds for modification (along with the safety and best interest of the child). The change in question refers to something that has changed since the previous order, whether that was in the divorce decree or a prior modification. Whether the change is material and substantial is a question of fact.

Mediation

An *alternative dispute resolution* procedure in which the goal is to resolve disputes out of court using a mediator, a third-party professional whose role is to facilitate settlement. Typically, the parties each participate with their attorney. The mediator does not make findings or rulings; their job is solely to facilitate a settlement. The proceedings are confidential, and mediation may or may not be faith-based.

Modification

An alteration of the terms for conservatorship, support, or possession of and access to a child by a court with jurisdiction, typically the court with continuing exclusive jurisdiction. The law of the particular jurisdiction provides specific grounds for enabling a court to render a modification.

Motion for Contempt or Suit for Enforcement

A lawsuit seeking enforcement of a prior order of the court, such as child support and/or access provisions. Remedies can include incarceration.

Motion for New Trial

A post-judgment pleading that requests the court set aside a verdict and judgment and grant a new trial. It must be filed within a limited time period after the entry of a final judgment. It is used not only as a means to have a judgment set aside and replaced with a new trial but also as a first step toward appealing the judgment to an appellate court. The filing and ruling on the motion are time sensitive.

Motion to Modify in SAPCR

A lawsuit brought to modify one or more parent-child relationship terms of a controlling *final decree* or a controlling *modifying order* of the court. Examples: Motions to increase or decrease child support payments or to modify in some other way child support provisions involving, for example, insurance coverage, payment of certain expenses, etc. Motions to change custody (the primary residence of the child). Motions to change access provisions or exchange provisions. Motions to allow a move of the child's residence outside of a court restricted geographic area. Motions to change a parent's rights and powers regarding issues such as medical decisions, school-related issues and so forth.

Motion to Modify, Correct, or Reform the Judgment

These are post-judgment motions that request the court to correct or change the judgment in some respect. Like a Motion for New Trial, these can also be used to preserve alleged error for an appeal to an appellate court. The filing and ruling on these post-judgment motions are time sensitive.

Parent Plan

A plan that sets out the proposed rights and duties of a parent, provides for periods of possession to the child(ren) and support of the child(ren), with the goal of optimizing the development of a close and continual relationship between the parent and the child(ren).

Parental Alienation

A form of psychological abuse perpetrated on a child by a parent trying to turn their child(ren) against the other parent. This is commonly seen in contentious child custody cases. Parental alienation is often evidenced by a child aligning with the alienating parent and showing contempt or even hatred toward the other parent.

Pleadings

Formal written instruments that set requests and the necessary elements for relief sought to be granted by the court or ruled on by the court. They are prepared and signed by the attorneys or a self-representing litigant. Examples include a petition for divorce; respondent's answer to the suit; motions for temporary orders; motions to modify in a SAPCR; counter or cross motions brought by the respondent in a family law case; motions to enforce; petition to terminate a parent-child relationship.

Rendition

Rendering of the court's rulings.

Request for Admissions

A discovery tool submitted to an opposing party that requires submitted statements to be admitted as true or denied under oath within a specified period of time or they are otherwise deemed admitted. A response can include a declaration that the statement can neither be admitted or denied.

Request for Disclosure

A discovery tool provided for by state statute that requires a party to provide to the opposing party disclosures set out in the law by a date set in the law. Required disclosures may include, depending on the jurisdiction, names of the parties; information regarding any potential parties; legal theories and the factual basis of claims or defenses; economic damages; information regarding persons having knowledge of relevant facts and a description of the connection each has to the case; and details regarding expert witnesses (psychologists, doctors, counselors, etc.).

Request for Production of Documents

A discovery tool submitted to an opposing party that requires the production of requested documents within a specified period of time.

Respondent or Defendant

The party responding to the lawsuit.

Ruling

The court's decision on matters presented in a lawsuit. This includes decisions on temporary issues, motions, and the trial on the merits (the court proceeding that will resolve the ultimate issues of fact and law before the court).

Split Custody

A common term to describe an arrangement where the parties have equal access and rights, typically with the domicile and residence of the children fixed to a particular county and geographic area respectively. It is not synonymous with joint custody, or the access necessarily awarded to each Joint Managing Conservator.

Standard Possession Order (SPO)

An order with terms that provide a noncustodial parent at minimum with rights of possession of a child (*visitation*) in accordance with a schedule typically set out in state law. The terms include provisions that address possession and access times presumed to be in the best interest of the child with variances depending on, for example, the distance between conservators.

Suit Affecting the Parent-Child Relationship (SAPCR)

A lawsuit that is filed with a court regarding the appointment of a managing conservator or a possessory conservator or joint managing conservators, access to or support of a child, or the request for establishment or termination of the parent-child relationship.

Temporary Orders

Orders entered during the pendency of a suit that expire when a final order is rendered or entered.

Trial Court

The court where the lawsuit is filed and will be tried. In some states, county courts and district courts handle most family law cases, sometimes with overlapping jurisdiction. Some jurisdictions have courts that are specialized to handle only family law cases, and some courts have associate judges along with the presiding district judge who typically preside over temporary hearings, and, in some cases, the final trial.

Venue

The proper location for a case to be tried (typically the court of continuing jurisdiction in a family law modification or enforcement proceeding).

Verdict

The decision of a jury on matters submitted to it in a trial.

Written Interrogatories

A discovery tool that is typically submitted to an opposing party through their attorney that requires a list of written questions to be answered within a specified period of time in writing and under oath (subject to the penalty of perjury).

Legal Terminology: People and Roles

Amicus Attorney

Attorney appointed by the court in a suit whose role is to provide legal services necessary to assist the court in protecting a child's best interests rather than to provide legal services to the child.

Attorney Ad Litem

Attorney appointed by the court who provides legal services to a person, including a child.

Attorney of Record

The attorney who signs the pleading filed with the court or who otherwise formally appears before the court on behalf of a party.

Attorney Staff

May include associate attorneys, paralegals/legal assistants, legal secretaries, file clerks and runners, and law clerks (often law school students). Associate attorneys are typically junior lawyers or non-partners who work under the direction or in support of a partner-level attorney. Paralegals or legal assistants are typically involved in client interaction and in assisting the lawyers in preparing discovery and preparing a case for trial. The terms *paralegal* and *legal assistant* are often used interchangeably and typically denote a person who is qualified by education, training, or work experience in the legal field to assist an attorney or attorneys. A *legal secretary* might also perform those same duties but is more often associated with administrative matters and clerical tasks. Many paralegals have attended a school program that provides education and training as a paralegal.

Child Custody Evaluator

A professional, typically a social worker, professional counselor, marriage and family therapist, or psychologist appointed by the court to conduct a child custody evaluation. In Texas, there are minimum qualifications set or addressed by statute to be qualified to conduct a child custody evaluation.

Guardian Ad Litem

A person appointed to represent the bests interests of a child. This might be a volunteer advocate, a non-attorney professional, or an attorney ad litem appointed to serve the child in a dual role (both as an advocate and as a guardian ad litem looking after the best interests of the child).

Lead Counsel or First Chair

The attorney who is *trying* the lawsuit.

Conservator

Managing Conservator (MC), Joint Managing Conservator (JMC), and Possessory Conservator (PC)

The label/designation given generally to a parent in a SAPCR.

- The *managing conservator* is generally the relationship given to the parent who will have rights to make most major decisions for their child(ren) and will have significant possessory rights (custody rights). The order might appoint one party a *sole managing conservator* or two parties *joint managing conservators.*

- The *possessory conservator* is generally the relationship given to a party who does not have primary possession (custody) of the child(ren) but has certain designated rights and/or designated periods of possession.

Parenting Coordinator (PC)

Similar to a *parenting facilitator,* this is a person agreed to by both parties or appointed by the court to help parents communicate, resolve conflicts, and make parenting decisions. This is especially useful in high-conflict cases in which the parents and child(ren) benefit from a third party's guidance and perspective. In most states, the parenting coordinator relationship is confidential to promote openness. As such, the parenting coordinator cannot be called to testify or report to the court.

Parenting Facilitator (PF)

Similar to a *parenting coordinator,* this is a person agreed to by both parties or appointed by the court to help parents communicate, resolve conflicts, and make parenting decisions. This is especially useful in high-conflict cases in which the parents and child(ren) benefit from a third party's guidance and perspective. In most states, the parenting facilitator's relationship is not considered private from the court, and as such, this person may be called to testify or report to the court. The parenting facilitator may also monitor compliance with the court's orders regarding the subject of the court's order.

Party

In a family law case, a *party* is a person, government agency (Child Protective Services, for example), or other third party who is a participant in a case either as an initiator of the lawsuit (petitioner, plaintiff, or movant); a named responder in the lawsuit (respondent or defendant); or a person or entity who has intervened. For example, in a SAPCR, a *party* might be a person not named in the lawsuit who is a parent or alleged parent or possibly a grandparent who intervenes in the lawsuit.

Petitioner or Plaintiff

The party initiating the lawsuit.

Respondent or Defendant

The party who has been served the lawsuit.

Second Chair

An attorney assisting the lead counsel at trial.

Chapter 1

WHERE ARE WE, AND HOW DID WE GET HERE?

Scott

Ding-dong! Ding-dong! Knock knock knock ...

My wife, Vanessa, made her way through the maze of dogs, toys, and toddlers toward the front door. Our living room was ground zero, the epicenter of activity for four boys—three of them age three and younger—and two golden retrievers. We had been married for four years at this point, and life was crazy. And we loved every second of it.

Until that knock at the door.

With a toddler on her hip, Vanessa opened the door to a man neither of us knew. He was holding an envelope. I'm sure the guy was perfectly normal, professional, and polite. In my imagination, though, I see him as a mob enforcer—a massive, thick-necked fellow, standing over my wife's small frame and thrusting the envelope into her hand as he snarled, "Here. You've been served."

Again, those aren't the words he used. Vanessa remembers him even apologizing as he handed her the papers. I'm sure he did. The papers he'd just handed her would ruin our lives for the next year. It kickstarted a descent into hell that I wouldn't wish on any family, as we embarked on a year-long struggle to maintain primary custody of our eleven-year-old son, Michael, whom Vanessa had brought into our marriage.

This wasn't a *complete* shock to us. We suspected something was coming. Still, when you are served those papers, it's terrifying. Vanessa describes it as "an assault on your motherhood or fatherhood," as you stand there looking at legal documents that claim you're failing so badly as a parent that the state has to get involved to protect your children from *you*. Your heart drops. Your fists clench. You realize you've just received your draft orders, and you're heading into war. It is not just a legal war, but a spiritual one as well.

The Bible says, "For everything there is a season, and a time for every matter under heaven ... a time to love, and a time to hate; a time for war, and a time for peace" (Ecclesiastes 3:1, 8). We prayed that "time for peace" would come quickly, but we were about to learn it could never come quickly enough.

Dennis

I spent a few decades as a tour guide through that legal battlefield, serving as a practicing attorney and family law specialist in the Dallas area from the early 1980s until I moved into an executive ministry position in the late 2000s. The combination of family law and ministry experience has given me a unique perspective on custody litigation, and I can assure you that it is a painful, anxiety-producing, stress-filled nightmare no matter which side of the door you're standing on—the one *receiving* papers or the one *sending* them.

Regardless of who starts the litigation ball rolling, and for whatever reason they think it's necessary, *everyone* is in for a bumpy ride that will lead to an outcome *no one* expects. In a custody-related case, a third party—the state—is introduced into your family dynamic, and that third party has the opportunity and the power to fundamentally *change* that family dynamic forever.

Whichever side of the lawsuit you're on, you are hoping for a particular result. But at the same time, you are putting all these key decisions in the hands of people who don't really know you or your family. The results can be—and all too often are—completely unpredictable. And, just like any other kind of war, you know a lot of damage is going to be done before there is any resolution. Even if you "win," you can still lose.

Oh, and there are no "winners," anyway.

Nothing can take the pain and anxiety out of the litigation experience. The fact is, though, that litigation is often necessary. Sometimes it is the only option available to ensure the emotional and physical well-being of your children. It can be the cleansing fire that burns away years of dysfunction and ambiguity, leaving a clear, workable plan that everyone can follow and is in the best interest of the children involved. Even when it is necessary, it's a battle no parent wants to fight.

Our goal with this book is not to make your litigation experience easy. Nothing can do that. Instead, our goal is to simply help prepare you for what's ahead as you jump into the fray. We fear what we don't know, and if you have never been through family law litigation before, you'll find out quickly that there are many things you do not know yet.

Most of us learn all these things the hard way by running headlong into them at full speed. Our hope is that this book will save you a few bumps and bruises by acquainting you with how a typical family law case works: who's involved, what the key terms are, dangers to watch out for, how the process flows, and how to navigate through all the difficult decisions you'll be forced to make. We want to take some of the mystery out of the litigation experience and give you the tools and education that will hopefully put you on more solid ground as you get started. We also want to help you avoid a courtroom if at all possible. That might be a surprise to you. Contrary to what many may think, the goal in litigation is not to get your case in front of a judge. The best outcome is to actually *avoid* getting all the way to a judge and a courtroom.

But now we're getting ahead of ourselves. Before we get into the reasons for avoiding court, let's get started by unpacking how and why people get into a litigation situation in the first place. If you've read Scott and Vanessa's book *Blended and Redeemed,* some of the information in this chapter will sound familiar. That's because we need to lay the groundwork here before we move into deeper issues throughout the rest of the book. That means starting all the way back at the beginning of the discussion.

When Is Litigation Necessary?

Why would it ever be necessary to change your custody order? Any parent who has been through a divorce knows that an enormous part of the divorce process is focused on the children—where they'll live, how often each parent gets to see them and have them in their "possession," who gets to make educational decisions, who gets to make medical decisions, child support obligations, and so on. In legal-speak, these issues fall under a part of the divorce called the *suit affecting the parent-child relationship,* or SAPCR. When kids are involved, a divorce is essentially two proceedings rolled into one. For example, if John and Jane Doe were to file for divorce, there would be the Matter of the Marriage of John and Jane Doe (the divorce), and in the Interest of Baby Doe (the SAPCR).

The divorce part of the proceeding is generally final and binding; it's rare for one ex-spouse to take the other back to court after the divorce is finalized. However, the SAPCR provisions of a divorce decree are subject to future alterations—usually due to either modification or enforcement issues—any time after the divorce until the child reaches adulthood.

Why would one parent take the other parent back to court to revise the SAPCR provisions? Most of the time, the reason falls in one of two main categories:

1. Something has changed.
2. The child's safety is at risk.

The specific circumstances could be anything, but any SAPCR modification case is likely rooted in one of these two things.

The legal term for "something has changed" is a *material and substantial change of circumstances*. As for what specifically has "changed," it could be almost anything, such as:

- The child has outgrown the original provisions. That is, what worked at age six probably doesn't make sense at sixteen.
- A parent wants to move out of state, out of a geographically restricted area, or a problematic distance from the other parent, thus impacting a workable possession schedule or exchange of possession arrangement.
- A parent is getting remarried and needs to plan around new family issues. For example, if two people get married who each have children from previous marriages, they might want to change their SAPCR provisions to ensure all their children are together at the same time as often as possible.
- A parent paying child support has had a substantial change of income and is able to pay more in support now than they were at the time of the divorce.
- The parent who has the right to make educational decisions for the child wants to start homeschooling.
- The child develops a medical issue or special needs that are not receiving proper care and attention at one parent's home.

A common term that is often thrown around in these and similar situations is *unworkable*. That is, the provisions granted in the divorce decree have become *unworkable* for some reason, which has compelled one or both parents to seek a modification to their original agreement.

Of course, just because there has been a change, you can't expect the court to grant a modification. The mere existence of a material and substantial change alone does not guarantee a parent's right to modification. The standard that must be met is, "Is the requested modification in the best interest of the child?" That is a high bar indeed and one that must, if contested, be proven in court.

Safety concerns are another thing that must be proven, but these are taken more seriously by the court and more likely to result in a *temporary injunction,* or orders that change terms of the decree or order on a temporary basis as you litigate the issue.[1] That is, the court might make immediate but temporary changes to ensure the safety of the child while you and your ex go through the litigation process. Safety issues that could trigger a modification case include things like:

- Emotional or physical abuse.
- Substance abuse (either the child or a parent).
- An overly aggressive or physically abusive stepsibling.
- The child is left alone and unsupervised too often and/or at an inappropriate age.
- The child is left to babysit younger siblings or stepsiblings at an inappropriate age.
- A parent lives in an unsafe neighborhood.

THE TWELVE-YEAR-OLD MYTH

While we're talking about reasons you *can* change your custody agreement, let's touch on one reason you *cannot.* It's amazing how many people believe a child can simply *decide* which parent they

---

1. Never make an allegation you are unable to support. And never *fake* a safety concern simply to expedite your case! Any quality judge will see right through that, and you won't like the repercussions for trying to pull a fast one on the court.

want to live with once they turn twelve years old. This is not true; it's a myth that has been around for a while now—and one that needs to end.

Remember, any modification to the SAPCR order must be *in the best interest of the child*. Even if a twelve- or thirteen-year-old *wants* to move to the other parent's home, that does not mean it is in their best interest. In fact, that move could be—and many times is—in their *worst* interests. A twelve-year-old child does not have the emotional intelligence to understand issues like parent alienation and emotional manipulation. An ill-intentioned parent may spend months or years subtly (or not-so-subtly) sabotaging the child's relationship with the other parent. They may talk up how fun it would be if the child lived with *them* instead, or they might try to convince the child that the parent they live with isn't doing a good enough job or doesn't love them enough. Then, when the child turns twelve, everyone is shocked that the child suddenly wants to live with the "good times" parent. What a surprise! Except that it isn't. In these cases, the child is just telling the judge what they have been told to say by the manipulative parent.

Even if manipulation isn't an issue, it could be a case where the "grass looks greener" to the child, or the child just assumes they can choose where to live once they hit some milestone age. If it isn't demonstrably in their best interest, it is unlikely a judge will modify the existing agreement. You could be in a jurisdiction where the presiding judge of your court, upon the motion of either party or upon the judge's own motion, interviews the child in chambers. But again, in such an instance, what the child has to say is only one factor in considering the child's best interest. And be careful what you ask for. With a skilled judge doing the interviewing, the child may say a number of things different than what was expected or hoped for.

Now, it *is* true in some states (Texas, for example) that the stated preference of a child twelve years of age or older is a sufficient allegation coupled with a "best interest" allegation for a modification lawsuit. In that instance, the child would express to the judge a preference for the petitioner to have the exclusive right to designate their primary residence. Certainly the child's wishes, for better or worse, become a bigger consideration in determining if the change would truly be in their best interest as they get older, but that still doesn't give them carte blanche freedom to dictate the terms of their parents' custody arrangement. Once the child is sixteen or older, as a practical matter, their wishes to change their primary residence of choice becomes a major factor and the allegation that the change is in their best interest is much more provable, primarily because it's quite difficult to force a sixteen-year-old to be somewhere they don't want to be—especially if they have a car or other means of getting around on their own.

Best-Case Scenario: Avoid Litigation Altogether

Dennis

Nine times out of ten, whenever a new client sat down with me for the first time—whether they were *initiating* the lawsuit or were on the *receiving* end—that client assumed a court date was in their near future. And in nearly every case, they were wrong. Most of those cases, in fact, never went in front of a judge, let alone a jury.

If you conducted an internet search on "what percentage of divorce cases go to trial," you'll likely notice two things. First, you will probably see that the entire first page of search results are from individual divorce attorneys' websites. Hooray for marketing. Second, you'll find that those law firms agree that the percentage of cases that go to trial is somewhere between 5–10 percent. That is in line with my experience as a family lawyer. This means that ninety to ninety-five cases out of a hundred are settled and closed without the parties ever having to go to court and actually try their case before a judge or jury.

However, depending on the dynamics of your particular case, you might still prepare your case exactly the same way as you would if you knew for a fact you were heading to trial. This would include the full discovery process and possibly having temporary proceedings seeking temporary orders, all of which would strengthen your negotiating position. On the other hand, discovery and temporary hearings might weaken your case, which is an incentive to try to settle the case as early as possible. This is where the advice of the right family lawyer is so very important.

Depending on which side of the table you're on in the case, the word *settle* might feel like a cop-out. I've had many clients who were so frustrated with their ex-spouse that they sat in my office, figuratively pounded their fist on my desk, and yelled, "I don't want to settle! I want to drag that [uh, let's say *person*] right into the courtroom and show everyone what a liar/sorry parent/no-account person they are! They don't deserve me making this easy for them!"

While I understood their frustration, I always responded the same way: "It's not about what your *ex* deserves. It's not about what *you* deserve. This is about what your *child* deserves. And trust me, that is going to be a lot easier to handle if we resolve this without a contested trial."

This is a hard pill for many to swallow, but the simple fact is that the court system itself will go to some lengths to keep your custody modification case out of the courtroom and off the judge's docket—and that's a *good* thing. A *very good* thing, in fact. I like to say if lawsuits were easy and didn't cost anything, our courthouses would need to be skyscrapers. Once a judge gets involved, both parents are essentially surrendering their decision-making power to the whims of a third party—the judge—or to the whims of a group of total strangers, the jury. I've had juries that fortunately got things right after hearing my client's life story in the relatively limited amount of time we had to present our case, but I've also seen them miss the big picture and get it wrong a time or two. There are many wonderful family court judges across the nation, and there are more than a few bad ones. Some will take a lot of time to get to know your unique family situation, and some will make bad assumptions and decisions to close your case quickly and move on to the next one. But whatever they decide—good or bad, well-informed or not—is binding. You'll likely be stuck with the decision that this stranger made for years, and it could (and probably will) change your entire family dynamic.

Yes, you can go through the time and significant expense of appealing your case to a higher (appellate) court if you think the case was decided wrongly. However, in a SAPCR, the judge's discretion is given great weight, and his or her findings and rulings are generally upheld. If you do get a favorable ruling by an appellate court, you will likely find yourself back in the same court before the same judge, trying your case a second time. Trust me, this is *not* something you want to rush into.

There are some significant downsides to dragging your case all the way through the court system and into a trial. We will discuss several of these in detail over the next few chapters, but here are some highlights:

- Getting your case in front of a judge or jury for a final trial takes a long time. It's not unusual for the case to last more than a year. That's a year or more of dealing with the stress, anxiety, uncertainty, hassle, and expense of ongoing litigation. Whatever emotional energy you have driving you into litigation at the start will likely be gone before your case ever sees a judge.
- These cases are incredibly expensive and could potentially destroy your family's financial well-being if allowed to run the full course.
- Your children will be stuck in limbo, knowing their parents are fighting each other in a long, drawn-out court battle. They could endure serious mental and emotional anguish as they

try to deal with the uncertainty of what's going to happen to them and how this litigation will affect their lives.

• No matter how long the litigation lasts or what the ultimate decision of the judge or jury is, you almost certainly will not get everything you want. If you choose to hold out because you think you'll "win," think again. Chances are, you'll just spend a year fighting through the court system to get the same compromise you could have had in the first month or two— only it will have taken exponentially more time, money, and turmoil to get there.

At every step of the process, whether it's heading into a deposition or using one of the trial-avoidance strategies below, *always* work closely with your attorney on every detail. Your lawyer needs to coach you on how to act and speak in every single interaction you have with anyone even remotely connected to your case. We cannot stress this enough—everything you do or say can be and probably will be scrutinized as part of your case. Do not take anything for granted. We'll have a lot more to say about how to make the most of your relationship with your lawyer in Chapter 3.

Avoiding Litigation Step 1: Work One-on-One with Your Ex

The first step to avoiding full-blown litigation is to do what may sound impossible to many people: sit down and have a calm, clear discussion with your child's other parent. Once a lawsuit is filed, everything gets more complicated, painful, stressful, and expensive. If you can avoid that by having coffee with your ex to hash things out, do it. One uncomfortable hour could save everyone a year of potentially unnecessary heartache and drama. You have nothing to lose and everything to gain. Just think through what you are going to say and stick to it, because anything you say can be used against you. A good rule to follow is to assume you are being recorded or even video recorded so you won't say or do anything that could come back to bite you if your efforts to settle matters are unsuccessful.

If you are *unsuccessful* at reaching a settlement, the fact that you at least tried to reach a resolution before filing suit could work in your favor. If you are *successful* in arriving at an agreement, you will want to have your attorney draw up, or at minimum review, the proposed agreed-upon terms and incorporate them into a modifying order to present to the court. A good attorney will advise you regarding what needs to be included in the agreement, which can sometimes be counterintuitive and could be statutorily required in order to be accepted by the judge.

If the one-on-one step fails or is not advisable, you might consider meeting with the other party with both attorneys present in order to enter into settlement discussions. Involving the lawyers kicks up the seriousness and expense, but this could be much more effective *and* have the added benefit of having whatever is discussed in this setting generally treated as inadmissible settlement discussions.

Scott

Vanessa and I learned a lot about the gut-wrenching legal process during our year in litigation hell. One of the most painful lessons was how hard it can be to rebuild a good, workable relationship with your co-parent after hearing all the crazy things they might say about you during depositions and mediation. We thought a lot about that as we wrote our first book, *Blended and Redeemed*. Here's what we said there about the importance of avoiding the court system if and whenever possible:

> Litigation can bring out the worst in people. There are days when you are sitting in long, drawn-out depositions, and you are putting your former spouse and maybe the new stepparent of your child in the hot seat. Then you have to sit there and listen as they potentially say horrible things about you. Things that are untrue, lies made up

Chapter 1 | 13

about you, situations that are exaggerated, and past mistakes or events brought up to paint the worst possible picture about you. When they're done, it's your turn to get on the stand and do the same thing to them. The whole ordeal is painful, heartbreaking, and embarrassing. How do you get past all that once the trial is over? It can seem nearly impossible to go through that and maintain any kind of healthy, positive relationship with your ex.[1]

Speaking as someone on the other side of a long and difficult family court battle, I promise you want to avoid this if you can.

Of course, I am not suggesting you simply give up, roll over, and potentially put your child in a bad situation. And I understand there are some situations that are completely untenable or in which it is impossible to have one-on-one communication with your former partner. There are other options for those situations, which we will get to below. All I'm saying here is that if it is possible to have a healthy conversation with your co-parent, try that first!

———————————

As Christians, we also want to take Scripture's guidance on this subject. The Bible has called us to work together to solve disputes in community rather than in the court system. Jesus unpacks the biblical ideal for conflict resolution in the book of Matthew:

"If your brother sins against you, go and tell him his fault, between you and him alone. If he listens to you, you have gained your brother. But if he does not listen, take one or two others along with you, that every charge may be established by the evidence of two or three witnesses. If he refuses to listen to them, tell it to the church. And if he refuses to listen even to the church, let him be to you as a Gentile and a tax collector. Truly, I say to you, whatever you bind on earth shall be bound in heaven, and whatever you loose

1. Scott and Vanessa Martindale, *Blended and Redeemed: The Go-To Field Guide for the Modern Stepfamily* (Southlake, TX: XO Publishing, 2022), 234.

on earth shall be loosed in heaven. Again I say to you, if two of you agree on earth about anything they ask, it will be done for them by my Father in heaven. For where two or three are gathered in my name, there I am among them" (Matthew 18:15–20).

According to Matthew 18, the first step would be a one-on-one meeting, with or without legal counsel. If that is unsuccessful or not a viable option, step two would be faith-based mediation using a Christian mediator or a faith-based professional counselor or parenting coordinator. If that is not successful, step three would be to submit the dispute to faith-based arbitration. Of course, we recommend relying on a skilled family law attorney through each of these steps.

Regardless of how tired or frustrated you may be with your ex-spouse, you want the legal system to be your last option. If your co-parent is unwilling to try working the issues out between you, or if you know you simply cannot communicate with them in a healthy way, then maybe you just need a little help—someone to bring the two parties together and manage the conversation. Fortunately, there are a few great options for exactly this.

Avoiding Litigation Step 2: Bring in a Neutral Professional

Depending on your state and local jurisdiction, the court may allow (or even encourage or mandate) the use of a *parenting coordinator* or *parenting facilitator*. These are distinct roles, but they perform a similar function. The biggest differences are in the areas of *privacy* and *authority*. The parenting coordinator is more of a confidential relationship, and the coordinator cannot be brought into the litigation process for testimony or depositions. For this reason, the parenting coordinator can feel more like a counselor, and the parties can feel freer to be totally transparent with the parenting coordinator without the fear of having their private conversations revealed in a deposition later. This higher degree of privacy can make the process more relaxed and therefore has the potential for getting more done.

Using a parenting coordinator can be a lower-stress alternative that can still lead to a result that works well for all involved.

The parenting facilitator functions similarly in resolving conflicts, but this person's work and conversations are open to more court scrutiny. There is no expectation of privacy with the parenting facilitator from the court's perspective, and the facilitator can be called to give testimony. The upside, though, is that the parenting facilitator often has more court-appointed authority to resolve disputes and instruct the family on what they need to do. This can be extremely beneficial to families in conflict who need an impartial third party to examine the situation and give very clear and binding suggestions on next steps.

Again, all of this depends on the laws and provisions of your state. As with everything else we say in this book, use this information to have a good conversation with your attorney about how a parenting coordinator or parenting facilitator may work for you.

Avoiding Litigation Step 3: Work Through a Mediator

The "final stop" before heading back to the courtroom is coming to an agreement using a court-appointed mediator. This person has one job: settle the case and get it out of the court system as quickly and efficiently as possible. Many parties go into mediation thinking they've got to convince the mediator of every part of their case and "win them over." Wrong. The mediator isn't there to pick sides; the mediator is there to resolve the case in a way everyone can agree on, even though the agreement will almost certainly require a compromise—maybe a *big* compromise—on both sides.

If you and your ex do manage to mediate a settlement, you will have your lawyer edit and approve the mediated settlement agreement. In some jurisdictions, this is treated as binding on the parties and must be accepted by the judge for inclusion in a modifying order, subject to the mediated settlement agreement (MSA) containing certain provisions that an experienced family lawyer will know to include. Be extremely careful here. It is very important to get the MSA absolutely correct before you sign it, as it can have the same force and effect as a rendition of the court. So, for example, you don't want to sign the MSA at midnight after twelve hours of mediation unless you and your lawyer have the clarity of mind to make certain the document, albeit a compromise, has all the terms you thought you were agreeing to (and doesn't have terms you did not agree to).

Of course, the options we've suggested above require an agreement and cooperation from the other party. If the timing is not right or the other party is not willing to participate, the court system has options that can facilitate a resolution of some or all of the issues. Additionally, there are plenty of speedbumps in place to keep you from trying to race through the process too quickly. If your divorce was finalized within the last ten years or so, there's a chance the SAPCR part of your divorce decree outlines and possibly mandates a court-avoidance process for you, including how you are to try to resolve future disagreements and handle modifications. If your decree doesn't provide a court-avoidance process, there are options available to assist parties in working through the issues at hand. Options vary from state to state but generally include the following:

- Mediation, agreed to or ordered by the judge, with a mediator that can be agreed to by the parties or otherwise ordered by the judge
- Court-ordered counseling with a licensed professional family counselor
- Appointment of a parenting coordinator or parenting facilitator (especially in a high-conflict case)
- Appointment of an Amicus Attorney, Attorney Ad Litem, or Guardian Ad Litem
- Appointment of a Child Custody Evaluator to conduct a child custody evaluation

One or more of these options afford you a better chance at getting a good resolution everyone can accept. In some jurisdictions, the court system won't even give you a final court date until you've utilized one or more of these options, so you need to take them seriously.

The court system will do everything it can to keep your modification case out of the courtroom and off the judge's docket. In doing so, they aren't just helping keep their caseload lower; they're actually doing you and your family a tremendous service. Jumping straight into court is extremely risky and circumvents all the wonderful provisions in the law designed to give you, your co-parent, and your child the best possible outcome. Even if it isn't specifically required in your divorce decree, we strongly encourage you to talk to your attorney about how to find and take advantage of mediation solutions. These safeguards are available for a reason. Use them.

Prepare – Execute – Recover

This first chapter, obviously, has focused on *not* going into a full-blown, year-long litigation experience. Sometimes, however, things are so broken, complicated, or urgent that a trial can't be avoided. And, of course, sometimes you're working with an ex-spouse who flatly refuses to do anything *except* drag you into court. If that is where you are right now, you need to go into the process knowing what is in store for you and your family.

That's what this book is for.

In the chapters ahead, we will guide you through everything you need to know about a custody modification case. We will walk you through each of the three key phases of the process:

PREPARATION

Everything you need to know and do *right now* in the early days of litigation, either before you file a lawsuit or immediately after receiving a lawsuit that has been filed against you. This includes understanding the basics of family law, the processes, the key roles involved, how to find and work with an attorney, and what to expect as you go through the entire ordeal.

EXECUTION

A step-by-step journey through each step of the litigation process from the moment you hire a lawyer, through discovery and depositions, and through the trial, verdict, and appeal.

RECOVERY

How to move on after your life has been turned upside down, reestablish a healthy (or at least *functional*) co-parenting dynamic with your ex-spouse, help your child heal from the trauma of litigation, and avoid ever having to go through the litigation process again.

Each phase of the journey is significant, and there are plenty of opportunities to embrace and mistakes to avoid along the way. So, if your litigation experience is unavoidable, it's time to get you prepared for the long road ahead.

Section 1

PREPARATION

Chapter 2

UNDERSTANDING
THE PROCESS AND PLAYERS

Whenever your time, energy, money, emotion, hopes, and dreams are tied up in the court system, you feel like you're at war. And when your precious little ones are at the center of that conflict, you know full well what the stakes are and who you're fighting for. It couldn't be clearer.

What's not as clear to us, though, as we go through the endless, irritating red tape of litigation is *who we're fighting*. Who's the villain of this story? Who's the "Big Bad" that's always working against you, meticulously countering every positive forward movement you make in your case and in your relationship with your child?

We can hear you now: "Are you guys crazy? Who am I fighting? My ex, of course! He/She's filing all these injunctions! He/She's burying me in legal fees! He/She's saying horrible things about me in depositions! He/She's poisoning my child against me! *Obviously,* the enemy in my litigation is my ex-spouse."

We understand. If you're in this mess, we know how likely it is that every fiber of your being is blaming the person who's either dragging you into court or who's left you no other option but to drag them into it.

However, as we begin this section on preparing for litigation, we need to start by making sure you know who and what you are up against in all this. This means telling you something that, depending on your specific circumstances, may be very hard to hear: your ex is not your enemy in this fight.

So often in family court struggles, we become so filled with grief over the loss of the former marriage, so shocked by the actions of someone we once thought of as a partner for life, and so scared about losing a relationship with our children, that we focus exclusively on our ex and never notice the real enemy hiding in the shadows. But you can never fully prepare for litigation until you first understand what is really going on: spiritual warfare. As the apostle Paul wrote, "For we do not wrestle against flesh and blood, but against the rulers, against the authorities, against the cosmic powers over this present darkness, against the spiritual forces of evil in the heavenly places" (Ephesians 6:12). Your true enemy in this litigation is not your ex. Your true enemy is the devil, and he will stop at nothing to destroy your family and rob your children of their joy, stability, and effectiveness.

In this chapter and throughout this entire book, we will give you practical, real-world, actionable strategies and information to equip you for the legal battle ahead of you. We'll tell you all about how the family legal system works and how to navigate it. But our first and best piece of advice as you enter this season of litigation is to prepare yourself *spiritually*. God has given us specific protections, pieces of armor, we can choose to "pray on" to get dressed for battle each morning, just like we "put on" clothes to get dressed for the day. Starting today, we encourage you to "pray on" each piece of the armor of God, just as Paul describes in Ephesians:

> Therefore take up the whole armor of God, that you may be able to withstand in the evil day, and having done all, to stand firm. Stand therefore, having fastened on the belt of truth, and having put on the breastplate of righteousness, and, as shoes for your feet, having put on the readiness given by the gospel of peace. In all circumstances take up the shield of faith, with which you can extinguish all the flaming darts of the evil one; and take the helmet of

salvation, and the sword of the Spirit, which is the word of God, praying at all times in the Spirit, with all prayer and supplication (Ephesians 6:13–18).

Now, with your armor in place and your mind fixed on the real enemy, let's get into how this whole litigation game is played.

Say Hello to the Modification Case

Aside from divorce proceedings, the most common family court case is almost certainly the *modification*. Because this is the central litigation issue at hand for nearly all the blended families we work with, we'll primarily deal with custody modifications throughout this book. The process we'll discuss—including each detailed step of the Execution section—is written with a modification case in mind. However, most of what we'll cover can be applied to other types of family law situations, and the overview of the legal system and terms should apply equally well across all different types of lawsuits that work through the family courts.

Now, what is a *modification*? In the previous chapter, we discussed how a divorce between parents has two parts—the termination of the marriage (divorce) and the provisions regarding the children (issues in the suit affecting the parent-child relationship, or SAPCR). The SAPCR includes decisions and court orders regarding conservatorship (parental responsibility), access provisions (visitation), domicile provisions (where the child lives), and child support obligations, as well as the rights, powers, privileges, and duties of each conservator. Because the welfare of your children is at stake, the legal system, with its mandatory provisions and directives, goes to great lengths in setting the stage to make these final orders as clear and binding as possible. Typically, one or both of the parties' attorneys actually drafts the order for the court to enter. So, generally speaking, each party should know *exactly* what their parental rights are by the time they receive the final divorce decree. And then, the court sends the families on their way with a brand-new family dynamic and (ideally) clear instructions for how to manage any challenges as the ex-spouses work together to co-parent their child.

This is all great until something changes. You'll remember from the previous chapter that the two main reasons for post-divorce custody litigation are (1) something has changed or (2) the child's safety is at risk. Remember, a qualifying change could be something as simple and unavoidable as the child growing older. As we've said, what works at age six doesn't make sense at sixteen, so it's likely that something in the agreement will need to be *modified* later on. That means, as much as most couples coming out of a divorce don't want to hear this, you should probably expect to face at least one round of modification litigation at some point after your divorce proceedings—especially if the divorce was finalized when your child was very young. That modification could be a peaceful mediation outside the courtroom; it could be a full-blown, year-long, ten-round fight to the finish in front of a judge or jury; or it could be anywhere in between. We'll talk later about what the entire process looks like and what potential "exit ramps" you have along the way. For now, it's enough to know:

1. Modifications are extremely common.
2. You should probably expect one at some point after your divorce.
3. Ideally, your divorce decree should already prepare you for future modifications by naming tools and resources for healthy future negotiations and conflict resolution.
4. Any modification will need *some* level of involvement with the legal system, as the divorce decree will need to be amended, filed, and signed off on by the courts. Even if you and your ex have mutually agreed to do something not provided for in your SAPCR, you will need to incorporate the changes in a modified order for the court to enforce it and for it to become legally binding.

That last point is important. A true modification is a binding legal document backed by the full power of the court system. We're not talking about an off-the-cuff agreement to swap Thanksgiving and Christmas for a year; rather, a modification means going through the process of making a change (in writing) to the SAPCR section of the divorce decree.

The Modification Process

In the Execution section of this book (Chapters 5–7), we will walk you step-by-step through a typical modification case, explaining each part of the process in detail. Here in the Preparation phase, though, it may be helpful to take an early, high-level view of what those steps are. You can think of this like previewing the route on your GPS before driving somewhere you've never been. Depending on where you live, how complex your divorce agreement was, and what kind of relationship you have with your ex-spouse, your litigation journey may not look exactly like this, but it should be close. Also, the process will be a bit different at the start depending on if you're the one initiating the suit or the one being served. Finally, as we discussed in the previous chapter, remember that you can (and hopefully will) exit the litigation process at any point by reaching an agreement through mediation or negotiations between parties.

Stages of a Typical Modification Case

1. Petitioner (the one initiating the lawsuit) hires a lawyer.
2. Petitioner draws up lawsuit papers.
3. Petitioner files the lawsuit with the court.
4. Petitioner has the papers served.
5. Respondent answers the suit.
6. Pre-trial motions and hearings.
7. Discovery process.
8. Negotiation.

9. Trial preparation.
10. Trial proceedings.
11. Rendition (the judge or jury renders a verdict).
12. Final order drawn up by the attorneys and signed by the judge.
13. Appeal process.

Dennis

Lawyers like me spend three years in law school and the first several years of our law practice learning the ins and outs of all the terms and roles above, and then we spend the rest of our careers using this lingo every minute of every day. Chances are great that your attorney will drop many of these terms into your conversations without warning, explanation, or context. Hopefully, you now know the basics of family law terminology, or at least enough to follow along with your lawyer. However, speaking as a lawyer myself, let me be perfectly clear: your attorney works for you. I've reminded many young lawyers working with me over the years that they are in the communication business, and it is *their responsibility* to effectively communicate with their client. If they cannot communicate with you in a way that you understand, if they refuse to slow down and explain things to you in plain English, or if they act like you should just trust them and "don't worry about it" when you don't understand something, you might need to find a new lawyer. The stakes are too high in family law litigation to "not worry about it." We're talking about your children! So, use this glossary as your ready-reference phrase book, but always make sure your attorney is communicating with you in a way that you can fully understand.

The Goal Of Litigation

We started this chapter by asking who the enemy is in a family court litigation situation. That answer (the devil) may have been hard for you to swallow. Now, let's close the chapter with another question that might be just as difficult for you to accept: *What is the goal of litigation?* That is, what do you hope the outcome will be once the dust settles and you put this experience behind you?

We've asked this question of many families going through litigation, and we've heard nearly every answer you can imagine:

- I want to make my ex pay for what he/she has done to this family!
- I want sole custody and the right to make all the decisions that impact my children.
- My children lived primarily with my ex for the past ten years. Now, it's my turn to have them!
- I want the judge to make them pay all my attorney's fees!
- My ex does nothing for our kids and doesn't deserve to see them!
- I want my day in court!

All these responses effectively mean the same thing: "I want to *win*."

If your goal is to *win* your litigation, we have bad news. You probably won't. And neither will your ex. That is because there are no real winners when it comes to family court. Almost no one walks out of a custody modification situation feeling like they got everything they wanted, and *that's okay*. Please hear this: The goal in a custody modification proceeding *is not to get the outcome you want.* If you go into it with an all-or-nothing, I-win-and-they-lose attitude, you are going to be constantly disappointed, deflated, and demoralized. Do not do that to yourself. Litigating over your children is already hard enough. Let's not add any extra hardship by defining *success* as hitting some arbitrary wish list of injunctions and concessions.

The goal here is not to *win*—whatever that means. And the goal is not to get everything you want. The real goal—the *best* goal—in a modification case is a resolution that (1) *you can live with* and (2) *that is good for your child.* If that sounds like settling for less than you want, that's because it is a literal, legal *settlement.*

We understand this is not the outcome most people *want* whenever they're facing off in court, so this is where we must remind people that it's not about what you want. This entire, horrible, angst-ridden experience isn't about you at all—even though we know it feels like it is. It is about your child. It is about making sure your child is safe. It is about making sure your child still has a relationship with each parent (or each set of parents) when this is all over. It is about your child knowing he or she is loved, seen, heard, and provided for. It is about getting to an outcome that, even though it's not *exactly* what you want, brings the crazy train of litigation into the station so everyone can get off and get on with their (modified) lives.

Remember, the goal is a resolution that (1) *you can live with* and (2) *that is good for your child.* That's it. That's the goal. You'll know it by heart by the time you finish this book, because we are going to come back to that goal a lot in the chapters ahead!

Take the First (Good) Exit Ramp

Scott

When Vanessa and I were thrust into an unwanted custody modification case, our lawyer sat us down and explained the legal process in a simple way that stuck with us every day of that ordeal. We shared his analogy in *Blended and Redeemed*, and we share it with every family we counsel on this subject:

> Being in a lawsuit is a lot like driving down the highway. Everything is going by so fast. Every mile or two, you come to an exit, but most of them are blocked and inaccessible. Even if you *want* to take them, you can't. But whenever you find an exit you *can* take that

gets you off the highway of litigation, *take that exit*. It won't take you exactly where you wanted to go or lead you to everything you hoped for, but if it gets you somewhere safe, take it. You may not have a better option—or any other option whatsoever—further down the road.[1]

Because our attorney set that expectation for us early on, we were always looking for that exit ramp from the start of our journey. It took us a year to actually *find* the exit that met the two key criteria (an outcome we could live with and that was good for our child), but we're still convinced it got us off the highway faster and with less wear and tear than if we'd stonewalled Vanessa's ex-husband every step of the way.

Now that we've laid a foundation in this chapter by explaining the key terms and roles you need to know at the start of litigation, let's shift our attention to how to find and work with the person who will be fighting this battle alongside you: your lawyer. We'll tell you everything you need to know about the attorney-client relationship next.

Chapter 3

LAWYER UP!

Many people think all lawyers are the same, but the truth is the field of law is made up of more than twenty different specialties: civil trial law, criminal law, bankruptcy law, administrative law, civil appellate law, consumer and commercial law, tax law, estate planning and probate law, personal injury law and, of course, family law, just to name a few. Every jurisdiction across the country is filled with excellent attorneys who are going above and beyond for their clients in each of these areas. And, sadly, every jurisdiction across the country also has several terrible lawyers who are doing the bare minimum. How are we supposed to tell them apart? How can we trust a stranger to fight the single most important, stressful, high-stakes fight of our lives on our behalf?

How to Choose the Best Lawyer for Your Case

In this chapter, we want to give you a framework for sifting through the field of legal professionals in your area and researching potential lawyers for your case. The key word here is *research*. You need to go into this with an employer mindset. Too often, we bring on the first lawyer we meet with or that someone refers to us, mainly because we don't know any better. We have a meeting, the attorney gives their sales pitch, and we ask them when they can start without ever meeting with anyone else. That's crazy! If you were hiring an executive to run the most important part of your business, would you simply hire the first person you talked to? No way! You'd research and interview several candidates, ask them some tough questions, check their references, learn how they've performed in similar positions, and pick the person who impressed you the most and seemed like the best fit. Hiring an attorney for your family law case is no different.

This is one of the most important decisions you'll ever make and, for reasons we'll discuss below, it's a decision that's very difficult to *un-make* later if things aren't going well. The goal is not to simply find a *good* or *competent* attorney; the goal is to find the *best* lawyer *for you* and *for your case*. So, let's talk about how to do that.

Hire a Family Law Specialist

As you get started, check to see if the particular attorney you're interested in charges for an initial consultation. Some do, some do not. You might factor this is in when determining who to interview. Then, once you're sitting across from them, you've got to ask questions to see if that person would be a good fit for you and your case.

The first issue is to make sure they are qualified to represent your interests in this matter. As we've said, there are several different specialties in the legal profession. You need someone who specializes in family law. This is someone who is highly experienced and has specifically trained and studied to work on the legal side of family relationship issues. Unsurprisingly, the "bread and butter" of family law is divorce and parent/child issues, but the field also includes things like adoption, surrogacy, prenuptial and postnuptial agreements, domestic violence cases, and child welfare issues.

Family law attorneys know the ins and outs of the family court system, they know (or should know) the judges who preside over these cases in your area, and they know many, if not most, of the other family lawyers in your area who may be representing the other party in your case. This is what they do all day every day, and they're good at it. Your best friend may be your business attorney or the best criminal defense attorney in the country, but he or she would probably be a terrible choice to represent you in a custody modification lawsuit. You wouldn't go to a podiatrist or an eye surgeon for your heart surgery, would you? Of course not. In the same way, you wouldn't go to a criminal law attorney or your business attorney for your modification case. There are specialties for a reason, so narrow your search to only those lawyers who are highly experienced, trained, and actively practice in this specific field of law.

Choose Someone Local

The next most important criteria is to find an attorney who is *local*. By local, we mean someone who *regularly practices in the court-house of the court that is assigned your case.* This is an especially important point to consider for parties who live outside the geographic area of the court where your case will be tried. If you live an hour outside of the presiding court's jurisdiction, for example, you want an attorney who practices *in that area*, not in the area where you live. Sure, this will make meeting with your lawyer a bit more inconvenient, but the benefits of having someone who practices in the same jurisdiction as your case outweigh the negatives substantially.

A local attorney is familiar with the local rules, practices, and procedures that vary from jurisdiction to jurisdiction and even from court to court within the same county or district. They understand not only how the courts in that area work but also who the court clerks and court coordinators are, who the judges are, and who the associate judges (if any) are. They've probably tried cases before those same judges several times and can tell you what you can expect from the judge who's been assigned your case. They also know or know about the other lawyers in the area. They or their friends and colleagues have tried cases against these other attorneys in the past and know their methods, which can help your lawyer prepare to go up against whoever the other party in the suit hires. Local family law attorneys should also be familiar with mediators, parenting coordinators, parenting facilitators, the area's social services, forensic psychologists respected by the courts, and custody evaluators used in that area, so they can better guide you through settlement aids and the alternative dispute resolution options at your disposal.

Dennis

At the height of my family practice, after experiencing many trials in many different jurisdictions, I had learned the hazards of "home cooking." You could also call this playing against *a home field advantage.* There are always benefits of operating within the same jurisdiction and with the same people day in and day out, where everyone knows or at least knows about each other in that community—the lawyers, paralegals, judges, court clerks, mediators, and anyone else who was likely to "touch" a typical family law case—and where it could be easy to anticipate how a judge would rule with a given set of facts or how an opposing lawyer would operate because the locals had all been there many times before.

On the other hand, being on the right side of a home field advantage is a very good thing. It doesn't necessarily impact the ultimate outcome, but it can certainly help as you prepare your strategy and build your case with nuances of the home field in mind. It also helps procedurally because you know the court personnel who control the docket for temporary hearings, or who set your case for trial.

Home field advantage often enabled me to share insights with my clients that someone from outside our jurisdiction wouldn't necessarily know. For example, there are some judges that are "Dad" or "Mom" judges, tending to subtly, maybe even unconsciously, favor one over the other; some that will lean toward a 50/50 access schedule and some who don't care much for that arrangement; some who are highly technical in their evidentiary rulings and some who are very lax in what evidence they let in; some who want a short and tight presentation; some who like certain expert witnesses; some who will more easily than others grant continuances (moving the trial setting); some who have peculiar practices in scheduling their docket and cases for trial; some who will rely heavily on their associate judge if they have one in their particular jurisdiction; some who have a track record of being persuaded by certain facts and not by others; and the list goes on. You must remember that the test of what is in the best interest of a child has a lot of gray areas and subjectivity. These nuances are important, and the appellate courts know it. Therefore, the judge's rulings will be given great deference by an appeals court, and the trial judge is assumed to be the sole judge of a witness's credibility in a non-jury trial.

Home court advantage has also enabled me to have a solid "book" on not only the judges and the practices of a particular court, but on the lawyers who would often be representing the other party. There's always "that" lawyer who floods the court with all kinds of extra motions and filings that are, for the most part, unnecessary, who is going to be viciously aggressive, and who won't think about resolving the case early on. It is part of their overall strategy to try to wear the opposing party down.

If I were representing a client and saw the other party had hired one of those lawyers, I would prepare my client. I'd say, "Listen, I know your ex's attorney, and I know how they work. They're going to try to intimidate you with a lot of random motions and allegations that will be both annoying and time-consuming. It's also going to cost you more money, because we'll have to deal with their litigation tendencies and tactics, and the case will either be tried or won't be settled until the very last minute. I am sorry this is who your ex chose, but don't panic. It's just how this lawyer operates."

There is also always "that" lawyer or two who is just plain mean and gets hired *because* they're mean, and there's the lawyer who shies away from a trial if the going gets tough. There are also lawyers who rub certain judges the wrong way, and there are some who play golf with your judge or the custody evaluator working on your case. The smaller the community, the more likely their paths cross at the country club, at church, or at the soccer field. That's all fine, but it's best for your lawyer to know these things up front, and that generally only happens when you choose someone local. An attorney coming in from another area won't know these things, so they will always be starting off a few steps behind and playing catch-up throughout the case.

Set Clear Expectations

It is crucial to set clear expectations with your potential attorney right off the bat. Too many attorney-client relationships go south simply because they weren't on the same page from the beginning on several key issues—the biggest one being *financial expectations.*

It is easy to sit down in front of a lawyer and pledge to "do whatever it takes" to win your case, but a good attorney is going to be up front about how much "whatever it takes" can cost. Chances are, you have no idea what your modification case is going to cost when all is said and done. If you're not crystal clear with your lawyer about what your budget is, you could be in for a major panic halfway through your case when your financial war chest has run dry but the case is still ongoing.

When you have your initial interview with an attorney, you need to come to the table with some idea of how much you will reasonably be able to spend to see your case all the way through to the finish line, whether that's a settlement or a trial through a verdict. With that figure in mind, have a discussion with the lawyer regarding the different factors and options that can impact the cost of your case. These can include (but are not limited to):

1. **Rates and Retainers:** The retainer and retainer evergreen requirements (more about this later), the attorney's hourly rate, and the hourly rates of all personnel who will be working on the case.

2. **Temporary Hearings:** Is one a necessity? What is the likelihood of having one or more considering that either side can request one?

3. **Trial by Jury:** Is it an option? Would you recommend it? What is the likelihood of the opposing party requesting one?

4. **Discovery (Including Depositions):** What are the likely parameters and options?

5. Experts: How and why will we need to bring in psychologists, counselors, medical specialists, and other experts? How much do those cost?

6. **Private Investigator:** Is one necessary? Why or why not? How much does that cost?

7. **Consultants/Evaluators:** Who else might we need to bring in to help our case?

8. We know it looks like a lot—it is. We're not trying to intimidate you; we just want you to be prepared to have this discussion with your lawyer. The bottom line is that any time your attorney or someone your attorney brings in to help even *thinks* about your case, you'll almost certainly be charged for it.

Now, let's dig into some of these things just a bit. If money is no object and there is an unlimited budget (rarely the case), then, yes, you would likely hire a private investigator who can look into all sorts of things. Also, you would probably take depositions of every conceivable key witness up to any limit set by the court, you'd bring in helpful experts and consultants, and you might even go to the substantially greater expense of a trial by jury. That last item is a big point, because it's possible that the lawyer you are interviewing has never tried a jury case or hasn't tried one in years. So, if you think you'll want to push for a jury trial, you want to know up front if the attorney you're interviewing is up to the task.

On the other hand, if you need to keep your case on a shoestring budget, it's equally important to discuss your financial limitations with the attorney you're thinking about hiring. Some lawyers simply do not like or don't want to attempt trying a case on a highly constrained budget. In fact, they may not even know *how* to do so effectively.

In any case, know that precisely predicting the cost of your case is essentially impossible unless the attorney sets a flat fee, but even that comes with its own set of risks. The problem with a flat fee is that it will either be too much or not enough, so you'll either overpay for the actual demands of your case or the lawyer will be stuck working a case for which they are being underpaid. You don't want to be in either of these scenarios.

Why is it so difficult to predict the cost? Because there are many factors outside your and your attorney's control that impact the costs of the case. For that reason, most of the lawyers you research will require you to pay their hourly rate.

Lawyers will typically require a retainer up front once you agree to work together. The size of the retainer depends on many factors, but it essentially represents what your lawyer thinks it will take to get the ball rolling in your case. They'll set that retainer aside and use it to pay their hourly rates and any court fees and discovery costs until the retainer runs out. Note that some attorneys, if ethical rules in their jurisdiction allow, may require a "non-refundable retainer," which means they have a right to draw down on the retainer before they have billed against it and can potentially keep the entire retainer even if the case is closed before their hourly fees and costs burn through it. This is typically not an issue, unless the case comes to an unexpectedly quick resolution or you dismiss the attorney early on, but it is something to consider.

Be forewarned: the retainer is likely just the *first* of several or many payments you will make to your attorney! Too often, clients will barely manage to pull the funds together to pay the retainer and then assume they won't need much more money. They are wrong. The retainer probably isn't even *half* what you'll end up needing to spend. If your lawyer asks for a retainer that would require you to sell everything you own and max out your lines of credit, take that as a sign that this isn't the right lawyer for you. You cannot let emotion drive this decision. You don't want the best attorney you can *find*; you want the best attorney you can *afford*. Otherwise, you'll end up having to change lawyers in the middle of your case, and that comes with a lot of other problems we'll discuss later in this chapter.

Once the retainer has been used up, most lawyers will switch to monthly billing, wherein they'll bill you for all the time charges and expenses they've racked up that month. Depending on the expectations laid out in your attorney engagement agreement, you might also be asked for another pile of money every time the retainer is used up to be used as an "evergreen" account to draw from. You can think of this as "refilling" the retainer. Monthly billing and evergreen requirements are both common; it is a matter of what your attorney prefers and requires. Whatever methods they require, you need to know what the long-term billing options are and they should be clearly set out in an attorney engagement agreement so you can prepare for the budget impact as you go.

Other expectations you need to set from the beginning include things like:

- How often do you want or need updates from your attorney, and does that match with the level of service they are able to provide?
- How do they want you to ask questions (text, phone, email, or in person), and does their preference work for you?
- Should you direct your questions directly to the attorney, or will you have a better experience working with an assistant or paralegal for day-to-day needs?

- Will the attorney you hire be the one who actually works on the case, or will they hand it off to someone else?
- Does the attorney have enough time in their workload to give your case the attention it needs?

Unless something goes horribly wrong, the attorney you hire will be the one who's with you for the duration of your case. You're investing in a long-term relationship with a professional, so make sure you each know exactly what to expect from the other.

CHECK FOR RELEVANT EXPERIENCE

Not only are there many specialties in the legal field, but there are finer concentrations even *within* a field. In the family law arena, you will find lawyers who are excellent at quick-and-simple divorces between spouses who have no kids; you'll find some who are amazing at handling complex property divisions in a divorce case; there are attorneys who are world-class in adoption cases; some are great at enforcement cases that are quasi-criminal in nature and can even include incarceration as a possible remedy or punishment; and, of course, there are those who excel at SAPCR and SAPCR modifications. Some attorneys are fantastic in all areas of family law, while others tend to stick to the same tried-and-true types of cases. Some are great at trying a case before a judge but not so great at trying a case to a jury. The point is, even when you are targeting family law attorneys, you still won't know for sure if the one you call first is going to be best equipped to handle your unique set of circumstances. That's why you need to research and interview several of them.

Scott

Having been through a custody modification case, and especially after interviewing hundreds of other blended families who have been through it, I've noticed a predictable pattern in what most parents do in their initial meeting with a family law attorney. The tendency is to go into the meeting full of detailed information and raw emotion and spend an hour telling the lawyer ever little facet of your situation. Right out of the gate, you unpack who you are, what your ex-spouse is like, how they've treated you, what you want, what they want, how your children feel about everything, why you're right, why your ex is wrong, and on and on and on. It's almost a cathartic experience. You may have been stressed about the situation and this meeting for weeks, and you might still be shellshocked from an unexpected lawsuit. So, as soon as you sit down with an attorney, it all comes pouring out of you. Then, 55 minutes into a one-hour meeting, you wrap it up with, "Have you handled a case like this before?"

Meeting with a lawyer to discuss a custody modification lawsuit is not something that comes naturally to any of us. We're all just doing the best we can. There are two big problems with this common routine, though. First, we don't give the lawyer enough time to talk. We treat it more like a doctor's appointment, putting all our "symptoms" on the table and expecting to hear a diagnosis. Too many parents leave that kind of meeting with an attorney signed on to represent them and having already paid a non-refundable retainer without ever hearing anything from that lawyer about who they are. We're entrusting one of the most important things in our lives—our parenting relationship with our children—to a stranger. That doesn't make any sense.

The second problem is just as bad: When we do all the talking in that first meeting, we spend most of the time convincing the attorney to take our case and leave no time to hear how they've handled similar cases in the past, what their success record is, what their processes are, and what their relevant experience is. When we say, "Have you handled cases like this?" we're giving them a simple yes-or-no question. If (or really, *when*) they say yes, we take their word for it without digging into the details of their experience. We can get so focused on hiring a lawyer that we forget the lawyer is also trying to land us as a client. They have a financial motivation to sign us. That's not a bad thing, and it's not greedy. It's just a fact of business. Therefore, we need to get more than a simple *yes* from them when it comes to their relevant experience. The only way to weed that out is to go into that initial attorney meeting with a strategy.

A better option would be to *not* go over every detail of your case at first. Instead, give the lawyer an abbreviated version. Be sure to cover the basics of your family situation, your relationship with your ex, your SAPCR provisions from your divorce decree, and whatever has led to the new modification case, but don't go overboard. Lay the foundation of the case, and then ask questions, such as:

- Can you tell me about your experience with similar cases?
- How often do you work with families in this type of situation?
- What is your typical process for representing clients going through this?
- Are your typical cases focused more on the initial divorce, or do you spend more of your time doing modifications to older and/or outdated custody arrangements?
- The attorney for the other party is <name>. Have you ever tried a case against him/her? What can you tell me about them?
- What is your experience working with parent coordinators, parent facilitators, and mediators? Who have you worked with in these areas?
- What percentage of this type of case do you settle versus seeing all the way through to trial?
- How experienced are you with jury trials?
- How long have you practiced in this jurisdiction?

- Tell me about your experience with different judges in this jurisdiction.
- Would any of your clients mind if I talked to them about their experience with you?
- Tell me about your assistant or paralegal. Which parts of the casework would you do, and what would you pass off to them?
- What's your communication plan with your clients in active cases?
- How often would we check in with each other?
- Who is your point person for communicating with your office?
- What is your current caseload? Do you have time to take on a case like mine?
- Would you work on my case personally, or would you hand it off to an associate attorney? What are their qualifications for cases like this?

You probably won't ask *all* these questions, but hopefully this gives you an idea of the kind of things you need to be looking for as you find the best lawyer for your case. And, just as important, this gives you the chance to hear from the attorney and to get a feel for what kind of person they are. This will be especially important as we get to the next tip, which is …

Pick an Attorney You Have a Personal Connection With

Your attorney will become an indispensable partner in your custody modification case. You will spend a lot of time with this individual, and you must depend on them to spend even more time working for you and fighting for your child when you're not around. This requires an unbelievable amount of trust. If you do not trust your lawyer, and if your lawyer does not trust you, then the relationship is not going to work. For this reason, an attorney is only a good fit for you and your case if you believe this is someone you can develop a solid personal connection with.

No, we're not saying your attorney has to be your best friend. In fact, we would caution you *against* hiring a friend or family member to represent you in a family law case. A close friend or family member will have a hard time staying objective throughout the case. They'll tend to become emotionally charged in an unhelpful way when you or your children are threatened. Your attorney's job in those times must be to keep their cool and, more importantly, help *you* keep *your* cool. That just won't happen if the person representing you has an overly close connection to you and your family. You need your friends to be your friends throughout this ordeal, and you need your lawyer to be your lawyer.

That said, you still need to have *some* personal connection with your attorney. You need to believe that person shares your personal values and can understand who you are, where you're coming from, and why you act the way you do. It's easier to trust someone to represent your best interests if they *share* those interests in their own life. If you are a Christian, for example, it could be extremely valuable to hire an attorney who is also a Christian. Don't misunderstand us; a non-Christian can certainly be a powerful and effective lawyer. We know plenty of them! However, as a person of faith, you may want to have an attorney who is going to bathe your case in prayer, who will act with godly integrity, who will encourage you in the hard times with the love of Christ, and who will seek the Lord's wisdom for every decision they make throughout your case.

Other personality-related questions you might consider include:

- Do you *like* this person?
- Are you able to connect with this person in a meaningful way?
- When you leave a meeting with them, do you feel *more* anxious or *less* anxious?
- How well is this person able to communicate?
- When meeting with this lawyer, do they seem interested and engaged, or do you feel like they're just "going through the motions"?

- Does the attorney have children of their own?
- Is this someone you can trust to work, speak, and act on your behalf?
- Do you believe this is a person who can work for the best interests of you and your child?
- Can this person relate to you well enough to "fill in the blanks" for you, keeping you informed of everything you want/need to know about your case?

This area is completely subjective, and it's something that can be difficult to ascertain after only an introductory meeting with an attorney. It will be impossible to be 100 percent certain, of course, but don't use that as an excuse to go against your gut if something within you is telling you to look elsewhere for representation. There are plenty of family law attorneys to choose from in most jurisdictions. You should be able to find someone you *click* with well enough to trust with your case.

Stick With the Same Attorney for the Long Haul

When selecting and working with a lawyer, always strive to stick with the same attorney for the duration of your case. Making a change in representation in the middle of a case can be a nightmare for several reasons. First, you lose a lot of time (and therefore money) by having to get the new lawyer up to speed on you, your family, and your case. Any headway you were making before the change, all the time you spent educating your former attorney on your family situation, and any trust you had with the original lawyer all goes out the window when you start over with someone else. Your case doesn't go back to square one, but your relationship with your lawyer does. Your whole case can feel like it comes to a screeching halt while your new attorney plays catch-up on weeks or months of someone else's work.

Second, changing attorneys in the middle of your case can look flat-out bad. It's not good for the optics. So much of a typical modification case comes down to perception: Does the judge think you're a solid, upstanding, responsible person who should be trusted with your children, or do they see you as flakey, indecisive, argumentative, and impossible to please? When you change lawyers, everyone's radar perks up. If you're on your third or fourth lawyer, alarms start going off in their minds. Remember, most of the professionals involved in the case probably have a long-standing work relationship with the attorney you just fired. If they know or think that person is a good lawyer, they'll very likely assume *you* were the problem.

Third, changing lawyers can give all the other legal professionals involved—from opposing counsel to court-appointed psychologists to the judge himself/herself—the impression that you're "killing the messenger." Good lawyers spend a lot of time giving their clients difficult, often unwelcome information and suggestions. When there's a reasonable settlement offer on the table, for example, a dispassionate attorney will be more motivated than an emotional client to consider an early exit ramp. Clients who are more interested in either fighting to *win* or simply fighting to *fight* don't want to hear about settlements; they want to take the case all the way to trial. When these clients get frustrated with their attorney's pleas to "be reasonable," they look for a new lawyer. When they do that, everyone else involved can assume the client is anything *but* reasonable.

Now, are there ever good reasons to cut your lawyer loose and start over with someone else? Absolutely. Reasons that would make us consider terminating a relationship with an attorney include:

- If you are in danger of blowing through your entire trial budget before you get to a resolution. As we've said, setting budgets is extremely difficult in these situations, and many families need to reset financial expectations after a few weeks or months. If you need to find a more cost-effective attorney for the journey you're on, do it. It's better to stay in the fight with a less-expensive lawyer than to completely drain your war chest too early.

- If you and your original attorney have not connected in terms of motivation. That is, you are each on totally different pages when it comes to your desired outcomes and what you are willing to settle for.

- If you've had a breakdown of communication with your attorney and have lost confidence that it can be restored. You need to be able to communicate with your lawyer; if they can't or won't communicate to your satisfaction, that's a good sign that a change is probably in order.

- If you experience a loss of trust with your attorney. This is a big one. For example, if they have failed to update you on key issues, messed up a relatively simple court procedure, handled a deposition poorly, have demonstrated a lack of integrity, or have shown a general inability to do their job at the level you'd expect, you should consider a change. This lawsuit will be one of the most complex and terrifying experiences of your life, and you must be able to trust your attorney to do their job with the highest levels of excellence.

Hopefully, you'll never have to deal with these concerns, but if you do, don't be scared to at least initiate a (potentially painful) conversation with your attorney. In many cases, the conversation alone will reset everyone's expectations and the relationship, and you can continue working together. Sometimes, if a change is truly needed, a different lawyer in the same firm can take over. Or if an assistant attorney has been doing most of the work, maybe a senior attorney in the firm can take over. But, if a total change is needed, all you can do is make the call as soon as possible and start over with someone else. You'll lose some time and money, and you might take a minor perception hit, but if it's the first and only time you switch lawyers, it shouldn't be too big of a problem.

Tips for a Great Attorney-Client Relationship

Hiring a great attorney is the first step in a long journey. Once you have that relationship established, you must *maintain* and *grow* that relationship for the weeks and months ahead. Otherwise, you'll risk having to replace your lawyer later or, worse, you'll risk endangering your case because you and your attorney can't work well together.

After guiding hundreds of people through their custody modification lawsuits, we've collected what we believe are the most important tips for a healthy attorney-client relationship.

PAY YOUR BILLS

In our experience, the most common relationship-killer between a lawyer and client is the client's failure to pay their legal fees on time. As we've mentioned, once the retainer has been spent, most lawyers begin billing the client monthly for all their fees and expenses. Even if the attorney has become emotionally invested in your case, you cannot and should not expect them to perform their job without getting paid. This is a well-educated, experienced professional whose skills are in high demand. If you can't or won't pay them (or pay them on time), there are plenty of other clients who will. This is why it is so important to budget appropriately throughout your litigation experience. We'll talk more about this in the next chapter.

DO NOT LIE TO YOUR ATTORNEY

We hate even having to say this, but do not lie to your attorney or attempt to lie in a deposition or on the witness stand. Never, never, never. Your attorney cannot champion your best interests if they don't have the *right* and *true* information or if they lose their trust in you. Being caught lying to your lawyer will almost always destroy your working relationship and will often cause them to fire you as a client. (Yes, they can do that.) Whatever facts you hide from your attorney will almost certainly come out in discovery anyway, and your lawyer will then be unprepared to defend you against the accusations. Also, in many cases, if your attorney knows you are lying while under oath, they are *required* by the court to either withdraw from the case or have you recant your untrue statements. Otherwise, they can be found guilty of suborning perjury and risk disbarment. No good lawyer will take that chance on a client, so do not try it. No matter how embarrassing the details may be, always prepare your attorney with every piece of information they'll need to do the job you hired them to do.

BE ORGANIZED

Your attorney—and your entire case, for that matter—will rely on the amount and quality of information you bring to the table. This will require you to take notes, keep a calendar, make a timeline of events, and maybe even start a journal throughout your litigation. The information you collect and maintain will be crucial to your lawyer's ability to do their job, so it's time to get organized whether it comes naturally to you or not. We'll talk more about what types of information you need to collect in the following chapter.

RESPECT THE SUPPORT STAFF

The support staff on your lawyer's team, including whoever typically answers the phone at the law office, will be invaluable to you throughout your case. They are a tremendous source of support, information, encouragement, and flat-out hard work. Knowing that, it is amazing how badly some people mistreat the support staff working on their case. Some clients will seemingly take out all their frustrations on the paralegals and legal assistants, effectively "shooting the messenger." Or they'll simply talk down to them as though their work is insignificant. DO NOT DO THIS! That assistant just might be running the show back at the lawyer's office. They are keeping your case alive and well; they're as essential to your long-term success as a nurse is to your recovery after surgery. They might be the one who is staying at the office until midnight organizing your exhibits or getting your discovery responses in order. Getting on support staff's bad side could be the biggest mistake you make in your case, so always be kind, courteous, and respectful, even when they're delivering bad news.

KEEP THE ATTORNEY INFORMED (BUT DON'T BE A NUISANCE)

Your attorney will depend on the information you provide, and they will almost always be happy to answer your questions, but don't drive them crazy with an endless barrage of calls, texts, and emails. Every lawyer has *that* client, and you don't want to be it. If something isn't urgent, make a note of it throughout the week. Collect each question or detail, and batch them all together into a single communication for the week. You should also ask your attorney up front who the best point person in their office is to receive your communication. Often, it will be the paralegal or assistant, which is actually great for you. This person is well-positioned and trained to sift through the information you provide and pass it to the lawyer in the way that works best *for that attorney*. But again, remember that the lawyer and his/her team is within their rights to charge you for any time they spend working on your case—and that includes reviewing and answering your emails. If they bill in quarter-hour increments, a two-minute text-message conversation could cost you a full 25 percent of their hourly fee. That's another reason to send several questions at once. You'll save a lot of money if they can answer all your questions in a single fifteen- or thirty-minute block.

DO WHAT YOUR ATTORNEY TELLS YOU TO DO

No matter how detailed, prepared, and emotionally invested you are in your case, do not forget that your lawyer is the one who does this kind of work all day, every day. They know what needs to be done and how urgent or important each task is. Your attorney will give you "homework" throughout the case, and they'll depend on you to get it done when and how they say. You'll probably be motivated to do some "extra credit" by adding *this* piece of information or *that* bit of research to what they've requested, but develop a habit of *asking them first*, before you spend a lot of time and effort on a task they didn't request. Your bright idea might be something they've seen a thousand times, and it may be something they know will be a waste of energy. There is plenty for you to do; just let the professional direct you on what that should be. We'll talk more about the types of information your lawyer will need from you in the next chapter.

The Relationship You Need (But Never Wanted)

A family law attorney is a relationship no one ever expects or even wants, but when you need it, it immediately becomes one of the most important relationships in your life. So, when it's time to hire someone, take your time, do your research, and use the tips in this chapter to find the best lawyer for your case. That means someone who is a family law specialist, who is local, whom you can afford, who has experience that is relevant to your unique case, whom you can trust, and ultimately, someone you can stick with for the long haul.

Chapter 4

5 WARNINGS
FOR THE UNINITIATED

Let's start this chapter with a quick recap of what we have discussed in the Preparation section. By this point in the process, you've become familiar with the process and the players involved in family court litigation. You also understand the true goal of litigation, which is to find a solution you can live with and that is good for your child. You've tried to avoid a long, drawn-out lawsuit by attempting to work with your ex-spouse either one-on-one or with a mediator, parent facilitator, or parent coordinator. You have at least started the task of interviewing attorneys and carefully choosing one who is the best fit for you and this particular case. At this point, despite your best efforts, it looks like you are, in fact, heading into a court battle.

Take a breath.

We know this is an incredibly scary and stressful time, but there is a pretty straightforward way these cases go, and we'll walk you step-by-step through that process in the following section, the Execution phase. For now, as we wrap up the Preparation phase, we want to outline five warnings we always give families in your situation. These are five things you need to know and start practicing *right now*, before you get too far down the litigation highway.

Warning #1: Do Your Homework

If lawyers and courts are involved, you can be certain of one thing: there is going to be a *lot* of paperwork. Your attorney should guide you through the legal forms, applications, and petitions you must complete or prepare, but there is one big area for which you'll need to personally own the responsibility: the raw data your lawyer will need early in the case to best represent your interests.

In order to do their job well, your attorney will need to be able to quickly get up to speed with your family history, custody arrangement, and any other detail that could likely be relevant to the case they're building for you. We'll walk through what types of information they'll need and the best format to use in presenting it to them below. In all of this, the goal is to organize the information in such a way that it tells a clear story. You want to make sure your attorney can quickly and easily get to know you and your situation and have a reference-ready tool to use throughout the litigation. Whenever a new claim is made or a new motion is filed, you want your lawyer to be able to get their hands on all the facts they need at a moment's notice.

This means you must do some organizational work in the early stages of your case. Yes, *you'll* have to do it. This is not as simple as just forwarding your lawyer a million old emails and dropping a box of documents on their desk. In fact, please don't do that. *Having* the information isn't enough. Your attorney needs to have the information in a format that is *clear and accessible,* and like it or not, *you* are the best person to put all that together. That's true for a few reasons, but it really comes down to *time* and *money.* No one can do this task more efficiently than you can, because you already know who the players are and which events seem most significant. A new lawyer coming into a case won't know early on who is important and why certain pieces of information are relevant. Financially, you will save substantial money if you do this ground-level organizational work yourself. As we've mentioned before and will discuss more below, your litigation journey will almost certainly cost a *lot* of money before you're done. Putting together the resources yourself will prevent you from blowing a big chunk of it unnecessarily at the beginning.

Your lawyer's time is expensive; you want every moment you are paying them to be focused on their legal expertise, not doing simple administrative and organizational tasks that you could do faster, better, and easier yourself. Yes, your lawyer's legal assistant can do a lot of this, and they might want to put the information and documentation in a particular format that's different than yours. But again, you will likely be charged for their time, and you can, in all likelihood, minimize the time they must spend organizing the information to their attorney's liking. After all, it is your life that is being laid out, and no one knows it better than you.

WHAT INFORMATION TO COLLECT

It may seem intimidating to figure out what information your attorney will want or need, especially if this is your first time in a modification case. To make things as simple as possible, we'll stick with four key areas:

1. Text messages and emails.
2. Photos and videos.
3. Timeline of events.
4. List of people with knowledge of the facts relevant to your case.

Let's break these down a bit.

Text Messages and Emails

Some of the most useful (and potentially damaging) evidence you'll hand over to your attorney is the history of written correspondence by or between you and your ex. This is *critical* evidence, because it shows exactly what has been said by the parties with little room for misinterpretation. A text or email *says what it says*, and it's hard for someone to deny it. So, you'll need to go back through your written communication with your ex and print out (yes, *print it out*; we'll talk about why later) all messages that could potentially be relevant to your case. This includes messages about pickups and drop-offs, any miscommunications, arguments and disagreements, frustrations, and so on. Print these out, organize them chronologically, and use highlighting, post-it notes, and tape flags to call out especially relevant information you want to be sure your attorney sees.

It's relatively easy to review and print old emails (assuming you haven't deleted them all), but text messages can be trickier. For this, you may need to take screen shots on your phone, send them to your computer, and print them all out. A better solution, though, is to research ways to archive your old text-message conversations directly to your computer. There are several options for this whether you use an iPhone or Android phone and whether you use Windows or a Mac computer. Conduct an internet search for "backup text messages to computer" to explore your options. Some of the best solutions may cost you some money, but it will make this job *so much* easier. When you go this route, you can usually export whole text conversations to a document format for easier, more space-saving printing options. Many of these software solutions will even let you export your old voicemail messages, which can be very useful if your ex has left potentially relevant voicemails on your phone.

Scott

When my family went through our modification litigation experience, we were very lucky that Vanessa had saved all our old phones. We were able to go back in time through a few different phone upgrades and collect text messages going back several years. If she hadn't stored those phones in a drawer, we would have struggled to prove some of the facts in the case we were arguing. Let this be a bonus warning for you: *save your old phones and text conversations!* Get in the habit of regularly backing up your phone to your computer or online storage solution and keep your old devices if possible. It's a bit of a hassle, but it could make or break any future litigation cases. Available software solutions can make it easy to create regular backups of your messages, so you'll be protected even if your phone dies or plunges over the railing into Niagara Falls.

One last word about collecting old texts and emails: don't *only* provide messages between you and your ex. Include any messages from anyone else who has influence over your child. That could include in-laws, aunts and uncles, grandparents, teachers, counselors, family friends, babysitters, and anyone else who has specific insight into your child's well-being.

Photographs and Videos

Photographs go a long way in telling your family story. They show your (and your co-parent's) involvement in your child's life, including things like birthday parties, dance recitals, sporting events, holidays, vacations, and so on. Pictures capture moments in time in a powerful way, and they turn you, your child, and the other parties in the suit into *real people* instead of just a case number.

For this reason, it's a good idea to provide a collection of photographs to your attorney that show your family "doing life" together. It also provides clear evidence of your presence at and involvement in key moments in your child's life to help defend against accusations of absence or disinterest.

Videos are also great and are becoming much more of a factor now that everyone has a high-quality video camera in their pocket.

However, videos can be a double-edged sword. They show much more than a mere glimpse of a moment frozen in time. Rather, videos put on full display body language, facial expressions, tones of speaking, and a variety of nuances that are lost in text and photographs.

Whether it's photos or videos, provide your attorney with anything you think is relevant—including pictures and videos that may make the other party look good (or may make you look bad). Remember, digital information exists everywhere. If you posted a video on social media or even simply texted it to someone, or if you backed it up to a shared family photo archive like iCloud or Google Photos, you should assume the other party already has access to it too. It's better for you to include it as part of your collection rather than trying to "hide" it by holding it back.

Timeline of Events

In addition to the raw data you'll provide through emails, text messages, photos, and other records, you also need to put that information in context by creating for your lawyer a timeline of events. This gives your attorney the story of your family, your custody situation, and the key moments that have led you into this modification litigation. This is somewhat like a makeshift journal. that provides a succinct record of your family story for your lawyer. (Keeping an actual journal is not a bad idea in case you ever need it, but be aware that you might have to produce a journal in discovery.)

We suggest going back as far as you can remember, or at least back to the date of the last order, and note any significant moments, both good and bad. It can also be helpful to go back in time prior to the last order and note major events or milestones. Use actual dates or approximate dates as much as possible and organize the record chronologically. Key moments to focus on include things like:

- Birthdays and holidays
- Special occasions and celebrations

- Family vacations
- Sports games, piano recitals, etc.
- Broken promises
- Traumatic events
- Drop-offs and pickups
- Major medical and dental events

You also want to pay attention to the details of events occurring *during the pendency of the litigation.* Everything is important, but the interactions that have happened since the papers were served can be particularly important. You, your spouse, and your ex are all parenting under a microscope during the pendency of your case, so keep an up-to-date record of events and update the information with your attorney every month or so.

You also want to keep the information in this timeline clear and factual. This should be focused on *what actually happened,* not on *how you feel* about what happened. For example, let's say you're a mother who shares a son (Tommy) with your ex-husband (John), and you remember that the father missed your son's eighth birthday party:

Say this: "August 6, 2021: We had a party to celebrate Tommy's eighth birthday. His father RSVP'd and promised Tommy he'd be there. On the day of the party, though, John texted me the following: 'I can't make it. Tell him I'm sorry.' Tommy didn't hear from him until their next regularly scheduled weekend two weeks later."

Not this: "August 6, 2021: John disappointed Tommy again by blowing off his eighth birthday party. He texted me the morning of the party that he had something better to do. I wasn't surprised. He's always doing stuff like this."

That's a pretty obvious example, but you get the point.

Do not forget to note the times when your co-parent did something *right*, either. This record should be complete, and that means documenting the good and the bad. In the example above, if the father showed up as planned, it is still worth mentioning. In that case, you might say:

> "August 6, 2021: We threw a birthday party for Tommy's eighth birthday. We invited John, who RSVP'd that he'd be there. John called me a few days before the party to ask if he could do anything to help. I thanked him and said no. John and I did not interact much at the party, but he showed up on time, spent time with Tommy, and stayed until the end."

The goal here is not to make yourself look good and the other party look bad; the goal is to paint an honest and accurate picture of reality.

Dennis

Here's a free bit of advice: Before creating this record of events, I strongly suggest you make it clear *on the document* that you are specifically creating this for your attorney in preparation for your case. This shows that it is part of your attorney-client communication, which should keep it confidential, undiscoverable, and protected under your attorney-client confidentiality privilege. This isn't that complicated. All you really need to do is include a note at the top of the document that says something like, "Dear Mr. Brewer, I have prepared this record of events for you as it pertains to my case. This document is meant solely for you and your team's use in representing me in this matter."

It's possible that your attorney will want to turn some part of this record into a demonstrable piece of evidence for a trial or hearing. If so, your lawyer can direct you on how to best prepare a special version for that purpose or have the legal staff do so.

Packaging the Info for Your Attorney

We don't want to make wide generalizations, but in our experience, lawyers like paper. They would rather have all the relevant material printed out and organized in a way that's easy to grab and review as needed than have a shared cloud-storage folder full of thousands of unorganized documents and photos. It's a good idea to ask your attorney early if they prefer paper or electronic documents, but in most cases, a physical record is a reliable way to go.

Keep in mind that your attorney's team, generally speaking, has to review everything you give them. And every minute they spend working on your case, even when you are not together in person (which will be the bulk of the time spent in the preparation of your case), costs you money. Therefore, you want to be thorough but discriminating. Do not, for example, simply forward them every email you've received from the other party over the past five years or copy a thousand random files into a shared cloud-storage folder. And don't drop off a few boxes full of random scraps of paper that *kind of* relate to your case. That just creates a lot of work on their end, and you will risk wearing them out. *Someone* has to go through all that, and you are the only one with the proper context to tie those pieces of information together to tell a story.

If you want to be a model client and give your legal team a head start on your case, strive to do this prep work on your own, print it out, and organize it into a binder with dividers and tabs that your attorney and his team can keep and modify as a resource. A three-ring binder is great, because it allows you or them to add pages and rearrange things easily.

You can start gathering material together even before you hire a lawyer. It could give you a perfect hands-on activity that keeps you focused, gives you something important to do, and provides an outlet for all the nervous energy you will certainly have in the first few weeks of a modification lawsuit. If you already have an attorney in place, check with them to see what format works best so you can tailor your research and organization around their specific preferences.

Don't Edit Reality to Make Yourself Look Better

As you are collecting the data for your attorney, be sure to collect *all* the accessible data subject to discovery—even the stuff that doesn't make you look good. Remember, the opposing side is doing this as well. Any public or properly discoverable fact or event you leave out to try to paint a better picture of yourself—a mistake you've made, a birthday you've forgotten, an insulting comment you made in a text message to the other party, an argument with your ex, a photo or video that paints you in a negative light—will inevitably come out from the other side. In that event, your attorney will be unprepared to handle it because you hid it from them. As we said in the previous chapter, you always want to be completely honest with your attorney about everything—the good, the bad, and the ugly. Your lawyer can only serve you best when they are armed with all the facts and information they need to both fight for you and defend against the allegations made against you. Withholding relevant information from them only serves to weaken your case and erode the vital trust between you and your advocate.

One final note about the information you give to your attorney: Your lawyer is obligated to represent you zealously and to honor the attorney-client privilege of confidentiality. However, they are also subject to serious sanctions (up to disbarment) for ethical violations, such as withholding properly sought evidence and suborning perjury. Also, in a number of states, the lawyer's duty to report any suspected child abuse or neglect trumps the attorney-client privilege. So, if they receive any information (even from you) that gives them a reasonable concern about the child's safety, they have an overriding duty to report that situation to the proper authorities.

DRAFT A LIST OF PEOPLE WITH KNOWLEDGE OF THE FACTS RELEVANT
TO YOUR CASE

Early on, make a list of people who have knowledge of facts you
think might be relevant to your case, and include their name,
address, phone number, and a brief statement about what they
know about the facts in the case. This will help your legal team
determine who could be important witnesses and educate them
about who might have knowledge of facts relevant to the case,
even if you don't call them as witnesses. This list will not only
help inform your lawyer but will also give them a head start if they
are called upon to provide a list of relevant people as part of the
discovery process.

Warning #2: Keep A Marathon Mindset

At the start of the case, there will be a flurry of activity. Things will
happen quickly, you'll feel overwhelmed and out of breath, and it
can seem like the hits just keep coming every day or every hour.
This can give you the impression that your case will be a sprint as
you run full speed as long and as hard as you can.

That is a false expectation.

These cases are anything *but* sprints. They aren't short, and they
certainly aren't fast. Nine times out of ten, once you're engaged in a
modification lawsuit, especially where custody or primary domicile
is the issue, you're running a marathon. If you don't pace yourself,
you will burn out long before you reach the finish line.

Dennis

I've used the marathon analogy with my clients more times than
I can count, but I usually add to it a bit: Imagine you are running
a race. You've run long and hard, your legs are killing you, and
your lungs are burning. Then, you round a corner and finally see
the finish line. You're almost done! The end is in sight! So, you get
excited and start sprinting, giving it everything you've got, using

the last ounce of your physical, emotional, and mental energy. But then, with just fifty yards to go, you watch as they pack up the finish line and move it two miles further down the road. You thought you were done, but the finish line moved just as you burned through your last drop of energy reserves. Now, with absolutely nothing left, you're stuck there trying to catch your breath and barely able to stand up. With nothing left in the tank, how are you going to go the next two miles that have been added to the course? And how will you go the three miles that might be added after that?

This may sound dramatic, but it is uncanny how close this imaginary race is to a long, drawn-out child custody modification lawsuit. Maybe your case will be the one in ten (or one in a million) that goes much faster, shorter, and simpler. That is unlikely, but you never know. And that's the point: *you never know*. You *must* go into this litigation experience with a marathon mindset and *keep* that marathon mindset until the case is truly finished, meaning new orders are signed.

Just because *a* finish line is in sight, it doesn't mean it's actually going to be *the* finish line. If you get excited, stop pacing yourself, and start sprinting, you'll run out of emotional, physical, and mental steam when they move the line.

The litigation process is filled with starts and stops. A lot of things need to happen throughout the process, and each one of those things requires a great deal of coordination, scheduling, and rescheduling. Most people heading into their first lawsuit mistakenly go into it with their eyes on a court date, but the court date is not visible until mile 25 of a 26.2-mile marathon. You've got to do a lot of running to get to that point. So, keep the right pace, slow and steady, all the way to the end of the race. And remember, the finish line isn't *really* the finish line until you cross it. You'll get there. It just takes time. So, as much as possible, keep living your life and try not to hyperfocus on the ongoing lawsuit.

Many people get into trouble when they finally get their court date scheduled and start focusing on *that date* as the finish line. In some jurisdictions, you get the court date very early in the process. That date can be months or a year out, but at least there is a date on the calendar. In other jurisdictions, you do not get a court date until you finish several of the intermediary steps, such as discovery and possibly mediation. Either way, keep in mind that the first court date might not mean anything. It could change multiple times before you finally see the inside of a courtroom for a final trial. Usually, all that date means is that you have your foot in the door, and your case listed on a docket. But that docket will likely include several other cases alongside yours. The court could push the date out a few times, or you or the other party in your suit might proactively take steps to delay things. Or *this* could happen. Or *that* could happen. You get the idea.

So, even when you get a court date, do not put all your eggs in that basket. Do not pin all your hopes and dreams on resolving the case on that particular day or week. If you do, you'll probably slowly go insane every time they move the date.

It is impossible to anticipate how long your case will take from start to finish. It is different for everyone, based largely on what your specific situation is, the attorneys who are involved, the county or jurisdiction you're in, how backlogged the docket is, the specific laws of your state, and many other factors. We hesitate to even put an estimate on it, but if you're in a major metro area, and if your case goes all the way to trial, a year or even longer isn't that uncommon. So, do your best to keep your eyes on *today*. As Jesus told us, "Therefore do not worry about tomorrow, for tomorrow will worry about itself. Each day has enough trouble of its own" (Matthew 6:34 NIV). That last part—"each day has enough trouble of its own"—is basically the motto for family court cases!

Because the process takes so long, you should expect to go on quite an emotional journey. You'll feel different ways at different times throughout the process. If you don't have a proper marathon mindset, you can easily burn out emotionally long before the case is over.

And you can never forget that this is also a long emotional journey for the children. They will not be as equipped as you are to manage those emotions over the long haul. Plus, in most cases, they will still be going back and forth between households the whole time. They will always either be faced by one parent or the other. It can be easy for them to feel like they never catch a break and that they are always stuck in the middle. If you and your co-parent are not mindful of this, you could unknowingly add insurmountable pressure to the children during a season when they simply cannot take it.

One final tip here: Do not allow your frustration with the duration impact your parenting. Never forget that throughout the litigation process, you are living and parenting under a microscope. You could have the strongest case in the world at the start of the litigation but completely derail it by something you do or say during the process. Keeping a marathon mindset helps you guard against those kinds of boneheaded mistakes born of frustration and impatience.

Warning #3: Litigation Is Expensive

Most clients want to know what to expect financially at the start of their case in their first meeting with their lawyer. Unfortunately, even the attorney will have a very difficult time answering that question. There are more variables than you would expect. A good attorney will do their best to put the cost contingencies into perspective, but you've got to know going into it that no one really knows what this will cost when all is said and done. The bottom line is that you should go into this expecting it to cost from several thousand to tens of thousands of dollars, and in some cases hundreds of thousands of dollars. Those bills won't only be coming from your attorney, although the bulk of them probably will.

Many other people, such as mediators, deposition stenographers, expert witnesses, and facilitators, will be billing you throughout this ordeal. Your lawyer will do their best to prepare you for this, but don't be surprised when some unexpected bills for expenses start showing up.

Scott

The families my wife and I work with in our Blended Kingdom Families ministry are always asking us how much they should expect to spend in their modification case. Sadly, we never have a good answer for them. Our hearts sink when they're sitting in front of us already scared and stressed out in the early days of their case, and we have to tell them that they will probably need to pull tens of thousands of dollars out of thin air in order to protect and defend their child and their parental rights.

I wish we could give them (and you) actual numbers, but the truth is none of us know. There are factors that you *can* expect, and there are some that are totally out of your control. Plus, you never know what the other party is going to do. If you're in a situation where the opposing party has more resources than you do, that parent can play a dirty game and require things that aren't necessary just to try to dry up your war chest. Or they can take action simply because they can *afford* to it: seeking various temporary orders, taking multiple depositions, or seeking a trial by jury. Furthermore, the cost is going to look a lot different if your case is mediated and settled quickly versus a longer process goes to trial, whether before a judge or a jury. All these different hits pile up over time, and many families find themselves in a financial nightmare *on top of* the litigation nightmare they're facing.

When your child's well-being is on the line, your first thought probably isn't going to be about your budget, but you *must* consider your financial position before you get too far into your litigation journey. The biggest mistake we see by far is someone engaging the best lawyer they can find at the start without stopping to consider if they can afford that attorney or, more importantly, *how long* they can afford that attorney. What good is the "best" lawyer if you have to replace them two months into the case because they are too expensive to go the distance with you? At that point, you will be forced to start all over again with someone else, and we've already discussed how problematic that is to your case (see Chapter 3).

On top of all that, I've heard from dozens of couples that the financial stress of their modification case put such an enormous added strain on their marriages that they feared they wouldn't have much of a relationship left by the time their case was resolved. Your litigation journey will be hard enough on your marriage; don't make it even harder by failing to take the financial side of your case seriously.

It is a sad but undeniable reality that custody litigation costs a lot of money. Your ability to come up with that money can make all the difference in your case. Sadly, very good parents can (and often do) get the short end of the stick in a litigation experience if the other party comes in more financially prepared. So, this is the time to shake the trees. Call in favors. Talk to the grandparents. Tap into savings. Get an extra job. Cancel your vacation plans. Check out lending options like a personal loan or a home equity line of credit. Trim your monthly budget down to the bare minimum and throw every dollar you can find into your legal war chest. And, more than anything, pray for wisdom as you set your budget and make your plans. As Vanessa and I wrote in *Blended and Redeemed*:

> If you're entering a season of litigation, whether you're the plaintiff or defendant, your emotions are a poor driver of decisions. Be sure to make decisions when you are calm and feel peace from the Holy Spirit to do so. Take a breath, step back, spend time in prayer, and make an honest evaluation of your work, your thoughts, and how much money you can reasonably afford to spend on this. We know that fighting for your parental rights and for the safety of your child shouldn't be all about money—and it's not—but the harsh reality

is that money is a big part of it. This will become a huge financial burden for your family, so go into it with your eyes open.[1]

Warning #4: Leave the Kids Out of It as Much as Possible

One of the most important things to do during your case can often be one of the most difficult things: leaving your kids out of it as much as possible. Yes, the case is *about* them, but they should not be *involved* in it. This is a matter between you and your ex. Always be mindful of the child's well-being. They did not cause this situation, and they are just as anxious as you are for it to be resolved. The last thing you want to do is create more stress and anxiety for them in a time when they are already enormously stressed and anxious about the outcome of the case.

The most common mistakes parents make with their kids during this season are venting to them or sharing too many details about what's happening. This can be (and almost always is) devastating to the child, and for good reason. The child is stuck between both parents. They love Mom and Dad and want to make them both happy. This can often leave them with crippling uncertainty about what to do or say around either parent. This is made substantially worse when one parent openly rants to the child about the other parent. There is absolutely no upside to this and there is an enormous downside.

First, you're putting too much pressure on your children when you use them as a sounding board for your frustrations. Your kids are kids; they are not adults. They do not have the capacity to process these complex behaviors and emotions in a healthy way. Let them be children! Do not try to turn them into little adults by trying to explain adult concepts or trying to justify adult behavior. They

---

1. *Blended and Redeemed*, 239.

can't do it. It will only leave them hurt, confused, stressed, and terrified about spilling one parent's secrets to the other. Children who have been through their parents' divorce and are splitting their time in two different families already have enough on their emotional plates. Don't make it worse by making your kids your sounding board.

Second, trashing the other parent to the child doesn't just bring more difficulty and heartache on your kids; it also puts your litigation outcome at risk. Judges are always watching for signs of *parent manipulation and alienation*, the ways in which one parent tries to sabotage the child's relationship with the other parent. They see it all the time, and they always come down hard on it. The parent who avoids this type of behavior—the one who is most likely to encourage and nurture a positive relationship between the child and the other parent—always comes across looking much better to the judge. It is a huge credit in their favor.

For example, you might have a mother who is wonderful to the children and is the best caretaker for them. However, her one flaw might be that she has been alienating the children from their father. Over time, maybe she has done enough that the kids never want to see their dad anymore. It is entirely possible that this one mistake could lead to the very unexpected outcome of the *father* being awarded primary custody, even if that isn't what the father was initially seeking! The dad might not be the best full-time caretaker, but the judge can become so turned off by the mother's alienating acts that he sides with the father. Can you imagine such an outcome? Well, if you're stuck in a pattern of venting to and oversharing with your children, you may not have to *imagine* it much longer.

Dennis

It is also worth noting that you should never bring your children to any court proceedings unless your attorney specifically tells you to do so. And even then, I suggest you get clarification as to why and make sure you heard correctly.

Occasionally, a parent will want the judge to interview their child. In almost every case, judges do not like to see the children brought into the legal proceedings unnecessarily. It can reek of manipulation and alienation. The mere fact that you want the judge to interview your child can work against you. You may think you'll win the day by having the judge interview your child and hear directly from them what you want them to say. However, you run the risk of having the judge see you as willing to use your children as pawns in a chess game you're playing with your ex. And indeed, if the judge does interview your child, it might not go the way you hoped regarding what is said, what is unsaid, or how things are said.

If your child's age and circumstances truly merit involving them, and if the pros outweigh the cons—and those are two huge and unlikely *ifs*—there are ways of doing this without seeking an interview with the judge. For example, the court can appoint a *guardian ad litem* to represent the interests of the child and speak for the child, or the court can bring in family court services or a child custody evaluator to interview the child and share their findings with the court.

To be clear, I am not suggesting that it is never appropriate to request that the judge interviews the child, but I am saying it should be very carefully considered and used in exceptional situations at best. If yours is one of those exceptional situations, *only* bring the child to the courthouse for that one specific meeting on the day and time the judge gives you.

Similarly, anytime you are going to court for any reason—whether it's for some preliminary procedural matters, a temporary hearing, the final trial, or anything else—*do not bring your child* along for the ride. Even if it is just for convenience or because they are out of school for the day, don't bring them. Even if you think you can just park them out in the court hallway or cafeteria, don't bring them. Unless you've been clearly instructed to bring the child to the courthouse, get a babysitter and keep your child as far from the proceedings as possible, and this includes bringing your children to your attorney's office outside of court. Don't do it!

Warning #5: Loose Lips Sink Cases

We just talked about keeping yourself from venting to your children, but what about venting to other people, such as your friends, your family, and your social media followers?

The more you talk to other people about your case, the more potential trouble you are inviting into your already troubled world. Yes, litigation is stressful. And yes, sometimes you just need to let it all out by venting to someone. But the last thing you want to do is air your dirty laundry publicly. That includes making nasty comments about your ex, saying sensitive things about your children, and talking about the litigation in general.

In a lot of ways, social media has warped our brains. It has caused us to feel this *urge* to broadcast all our private thoughts and feelings to the world. But even before the days of Twitter, Instagram, and TikTok, people got pretty comfortable airing their dirty laundry using old-school gossiping technologies like the telephone and dinner parties. We tend do this because we are looking for reinforcement. We want our friends and "followers" to take our side, to agree with us, and support us no matter what. So, we offer our version of what's happening. We tell everyone we know about our case. We post barbs about our ex online. We create a little echo chamber where *we're* right and *they're* wrong. And we feel safe, because, after all, we're only telling our friends and, of course, the people who like us enough to follow our social media accounts. What's the problem?

The problem is that in a litigation situation, any comment can be taken a number of different ways by people who are outside our circle—and you can be certain that these things will, in fact, be seen and heard by people you didn't want or expect to include.

Telling a bunch of people in real life is dangerous enough, but posting anything about your case on social media is a disaster waiting to happen. Anything you say or do on social media (and via text messages, for that matter), does not belong to you anymore. It has effectively been broadcast to the entire world. You cannot control who sees it, how they interpret it, and what they do with it. That is the nature of social media.

It doesn't matter what privacy settings you have on your account. You may have your posts set to be visible to friends only, but there's a good chance you and your ex have friends in common. Someone could take a screenshot of something you say and send it to your ex, and then you're shocked when it shows up in court. You need to expect that. Just assume that there are spies everywhere, both in your list of followers and in your real-world friend groups. And those "spies" may not be malicious. Don't forget that *anyone* could potentially be subpoenaed to give a deposition to the court. That means anything you've told your best friend in confidence could potentially be pulled out of them in their sworn testimony. And when they are under oath, they *must* answer honestly and completely. It's unfair to expect someone to perjure themselves for you, and it could very likely hurt your case even more if they do. It's a lose-lose situation for you both.

So, before you put anything on social media, send an especially snarky text message to a friend, or tell the whole sordid story to someone over coffee, ask yourself these questions:

- How is it going to feel if I have to read this aloud in front of a judge or jury?
- How will that make me look to the court?
- How will that work in the best interest of my children?
- How will this help us reach a settlement more quickly and more easily?

That last question is so important, and it should be *the* deciding factor when you're wondering if what you are about to say is "safe" or not. Whether it is social media, text messages, or gossip in your backyard, always remember that your chief goal in litigation is not to antagonize the other party for the sake of making yourself feel better. The goal is not to prove what a great parent you are and how bad the other parent is. The goal isn't even to "win" your case. The only real goal, as we've said many times, is a resolution you can live with and is best for your children. Anything you are doing or saying that is not in service of that goal is probably taking you further from it.

Of course, you are going to need to talk to *someone* throughout the process. We aren't saying you should bottle everything up and try not to explode for the entire length of the case. We're just saying you should be careful and judicious in whom you talk to, what you say, and how much you reveal. We'd also recommend that you have these conversations in person, rather than by email or text messages. The person you are talking to could certainly be deposed and asked about the content of the conversation, but that is still better for you than if text messages, emails, or social media posts in your own words are brought into evidence.

You can also make use of privileged individuals to talk to who *can't* be called on testify. This obviously includes your attorney, but your attorney won't be the best person to help you carry the emotional burden. Talk to your attorney about what kind of safe, privileged resources are available to you to let off some steam in a healthy but protected way.

The Time of Preparation Is Over

If you've come this far and are still certain you are heading into full-blown litigation, then it's time to buckle up. As bumpy as the road has been so far, it's about to get much, much worse. But don't freak out! If you're the one about to file the lawsuit and initiate the litigation, remember that you are doing this for a good reason. You've identified a material and substantial change in your family situation that requires a modification, and you're prepared to take those difficult steps for the sake of your child. It will be a challenging season, but the result should be an arrangement that is a better, more comfortable fit for your child. And if you are the one who's been served papers or you think you might be served soon, remember that the process ahead, as tough as it can be, is specifically designed to find the best outcome for your child—regardless of the motivations of the person who filed the lawsuit. Even if your ex has served you papers and is making big claims about what he or she is about to put you through, you and your child could still come out ahead on this thing.

With that said, the time of preparation has come to an end. Now, it's time to execute the lawsuit, following the (mostly) clear steps through the litigation journey ahead.

Section 2

EXECUTION

Chapter 5

THE PRE-TRIAL FIRESTORM

When you're lost on a road trip, on a hiking trail, or in a shopping mall, few things bring as much relief as a giant map with a big red arrow and those three magic words: *You Are Here*. If you know where you are and where you are within the context of the larger journey you're on, you feel *some* sense of control. You may be in unfamiliar territory, but at least you are not lost anymore. It may not make the journey any *easier*, but it makes it feel a bit more *manageable*. And sometimes, that's all you need to be able to keep moving forward.

That's what we want this section of the book, Execution, to be for you: your great, big red *You Are Here* arrow marking your current location on the litigation map. As scary and complex as this process may seem, most modification cases follow the same basic pattern. And even though this may be your first time going through it, everyone else involved—the lawyers, judges, mediators, parent facilitators, psychologists, etc.—have done this many times already. They know this world and, more importantly, they know how to navigate it. You are not alone.

At this stage of the process, your attempts at avoiding litigation haven't panned out, and it looks like you are heading into a full-blown lawsuit. This thing is happening whether you want it to or not. So, let's get ready for it.

How to Use This Section of the Book

In Chapter 2, we gave you a list of 13 stages of a typical modification case. Now, over the next few chapters, we will walk you through each stage in detail, explaining exactly what's happening, who's doing what, what's required, and what you need to know for each step of the journey. We know from experience that the biggest fear heading into these cases is simply facing the unknown, so we're going to do our best to demystify things for you. The steps we'll examine will vary a bit depending on your state and if you are the one initiating the suit (the *petitioner*) or the one being served (the *respondent*), but this process is fairly standard and predictable.

At the start of each of these Execution chapters, we'll show you the full list of stages and call out the ones we will cover in that chapter—your *You Are Here* indicator. Here, in this chapter, we'll examine the first three stages of the process, what we call the *pre-trial firestorm*. These three steps represent what the petitioner is doing behind the scenes to put the case in motion. Even if you're not the one initiating the lawsuit, it will be helpful for you to know what the other party in your case has done before serving you papers.

Stages of a Typical Modification Case

1. Petitioner (the one initiating the lawsuit) hires a lawyer.

2. Petitioner draws up lawsuit papers.

3. Petitioner files the lawsuit with the court.

You are here

4. Petitioner has the papers served.

5. Respondent answers the suit.

6. Pre-trial motions and hearings.

7. Discovery process.

8. Negotiation.

9. Trial preparation.

10. Trial proceedings.

11. Rendition (the judge or jury renders a verdict).

12. Final order drawn up by the attorneys and signed by the judge.

13. Appeal process.

Execution Phase Step 1: Hire a Lawyer

If you think you need to initiate a modification lawsuit, the first step should be obvious: hire a lawyer. We already talked about finding, hiring, and working with your attorney in detail in Chapter 3, so there's no need to say much here.

The bottom line is that a quality attorney will be indispensable as you go through this ordeal. Yes, you can handle all the filings, motions, and pleadings without a lawyer, but we absolutely do not recommend trying to do this on your own unless it is completely unavoidable from a financial standpoint. Your parental rights and the well-being of your child(ren) are at stake here. If there is *anything* you can do to have a good lawyer at your side, do it.

Execution Phase Step 2: Draw Up Papers

If this is your first time in a litigation situation (aside from divorce), the term *papers* can seem oddly terrifying. Some people use the term *papers* as a threat saying things like, "Don't be surprised if you get served papers sometime soon." When a marriage is coming to an end, couples tend to use the term *divorce*. When they're taking their ex-spouse back to court over a custody modification, many parents simply use the term *papers*, as if the paperwork itself was the problem. It is strange, but strangely common.

So, what's all the fuss about these "papers"? What's in them, how do you draw them up, and what makes them so scary? Let's break it down.

"Drawing up papers" is just another way to say someone is preparing to file a *pleading* with the court. This *pleading* is the paperwork that initiates a lawsuit. The party filing the pleading is called the *petitioner*, or sometimes the *movant*. In your current situation as you read this, you might be the petitioner or the respondent (the person being served), but for simplicity, we'll explain this from the perspective of the petitioner.

As much as we as parents dread either serving or being served custody modification papers, the pleading itself can be surprisingly short and simple. It amounts to little more than a standard three- to six-page form that your lawyer has filled out many times. The pleading will generally include a brief response to several key pieces of information, including:

1. Parties and Children

The pleading will specify who the petitioner is, who the respondent is, and the names, sex, and birthdates of the children involved. It will also include information on where each party lives, the children's primary residence, and any other information needed to clarify who's who in the case.

2. COURT WITH JURISDICTION

The pleading will state the court that has the legal authority to rule on your case. In most cases, the starting point will be the *court of continuing jurisdiction* that is named in your divorce decree. If all parties still live in the same area you lived in at the time of your divorce, the same court that ruled over your divorce case will likely rule over your modification. However, if the parties have since moved outside that court's jurisdiction, your lawyer will likely need to file a motion to have your modification case transferred to the jurisdiction where you currently live. If you and your ex live in different areas, your lawyer will need to advise you on which jurisdiction would be most appropriate for your case (but it will likely be the jurisdiction of your child's primary residence).

As a reminder, it's always best to hire a lawyer who works in the jurisdiction where your case will be tried. So, if your case is transferred to another jurisdiction after you've hired your attorney, be sure to ask him or her if they've tried many cases in the new jurisdiction. If not, you might consider finding a new lawyer who's more familiar with that specific jurisdiction before your case really gets moving. As we've said, it will be much harder and riskier to change attorneys later.

3. THE PRIOR ORDER

The starting point for any modification is, of course, the prior order, or the current custody arrangement per the most recent court order. If this is your first modification litigation, the prior order will be the SAPCR details in your divorce decree. If you've been through a modification case before, the ruling from that case will be the prior order.

Be aware that, unless there is a pressing situation that requires the court to issue temporary orders (such as a clear risk to the child's health or safety), the arrangement set forth in the prior order will remain in force throughout the duration of your modification case—no matter how long it takes. It's also worth noting that you want to be extremely compliant with those orders throughout your case. Again, you are parenting under a microscope throughout your modification litigation, so be careful not to violate the provisions in the order that are in place as you petition the court to modify them.

4. GROUNDS

The pleading should contain grounds that the law requires to be proved in order to modify the existing, controlling, court order. To start, it will likely allege that the requested modification is in the best interest of the child. Beyond that, the allegations contained in the pleading will depend upon various sets of circumstances, the specific type of modification being requested, and whether the court is being asked to issue any number of immediate relief or temporary orders that would be in effect during the pendency of the suit.

For example, a typical pleading seeking a change of custody or a change of the primary residence of the child would allege either

1. that there has been a material and substantial change of circumstances since the prior order was rendered;

2. that the child is at least twelve years of age and will express to the court in chambers the name of the person who is the child's preference to have the exclusive right to designate the primary residence of the child;

3. the conservator who has the exclusive right to designate the primary residence of the child has voluntarily relinquished the primary care and possession of the child to another person for at least six months;

and that the requested modification would be in the best interest of the child. If *ex parte* relief is being requested (meaning you're asking the court to take immediate action without first consulting the other party), or if the court is being requested to enter temporary orders, there will likely be specific allegations to support such relief in an accompanying affidavit.

It should also be noted that the key words here are *material and substantial.* You can't take your ex back to court just because something has changed, such as, "My ex-husband moved into a new house 10 minutes further away." The change has to be *material and substantial,* meaning it's a major change that directly impacts your child's well-being or the prior custody orders.

It's important to note here that *grounds* does not mean *a list of everything your ex has done wrong.* If you've been following our suggestions for the Preparation phase, you might have already started working on your timeline of events as discussed in the previous chapter. In that phase, it is important to record the relevant details of your ex's parenting, actions, and behavior. However, the pleading is *not* the place to dump all that information, no matter how dramatic and compelling it may be. The only exception to this is if, as mentioned, you are seeking extraordinary relief in the form of temporary orders or *ex parte* orders, in which case you will likely be required to set out supporting allegations in the form of a sworn affidavit that your attorney will help you prepare.

Dennis

Often I've had clients who spent weeks creating a huge record of events that outlined every mistake and misstep their ex-spouse had made for the past five years. Armed with all that information, they met with me in my office for two or three hours, going through all the *gotchas* they noted in their prep work in meticulous detail. Then, when they saw the pleading I prepared to file with the court afterward, they called me, perplexed that I barely included anything they told me. They might say something like, "You didn't say anything about *this!* You didn't include *that!* This document barely says anything about what my ex has said and done to me and my children! Weren't you listening to me?!"

I get it. By the time someone is ready to draw up papers to take their ex back to court, emotions are running high. And there may be some excellent reasons to initiate a lawsuit. But, as I explain to my clients, the pleading is not the place to argue the case. The pleading is simply the first knock on the court's door. It is not the case; it is the *bones* of your case. It is the instrument by which the law requires you to give notice of the relief you are requesting from the court and the grounds you are relying on to support that relief.

Piling too much information and too many specific allegations into the pleading is a mistake for several reasons. First and foremost, it is unnecessary and inappropriate at this stage. You are not making your case in the pleading; rather, you're alerting the court and your ex that you're *about* to make your case through the course of the litigation, setting out the changes you are requesting the court to make and the legal grounds that support your requests. It may not feel very satisfying, but that's really all the pleading is. It is the starting line of the litigation race—which, you'll remember, is a marathon. You'll have plenty of opportunity to bring in all the facts and evidence and make all your arguments *when the proper time comes.*

Second, the law does not favor the inclusion of specific facts in your pleading. Providing too much detail at this stage might cause some blowback, and your lawyer could be called to the courthouse to defend their decision to include so much. This also gives the opposing party an open door to an immediate objection, which would likely cause you to have to amend your pleading to remove specific allegations. You could even end up having to pay your ex's legal fees for their lawyer's time in correcting your over-done pleading.

Remember too, that whatever you put in your pleadings and file at the courthouse becomes a public record and available to the general public. This means anyone—including your children once they become adults—can view the pleading filed with the court. These days, many jurisdictions even make public documents, like pleadings, available for anyone to peruse online. You should give some thought to what family business you want to put out there for the world to see now or in years to come.

Your attorney will guide you on what grounds and allegations are appropriate for the pleading given your particular set of circumstances. Trust that guidance; you are paying a lot of money for it.

5. Relief/Modification You Are Seeking

Next, the pleading will state the relief or modification you are seeking from the court. It could be a change in visitation, child support, or primary residence, or it could be something like permission to move the child(ren) further away from the other party than the prior order allows. The relief is basically what you hope to get out of this litigation.

You need to look at this in terms of two levels. First, you'll probably discuss the finer details in your early meetings with your attorney. It is perfectly understandable and appropriate to lay out the details of your situation to your lawyer and ask questions, such as:

- What should we ask for?
- What would be fair and equitable in this situation?
- What would be the best long-term solution that's in the best interest of my child?
- Is *this* too little? Is *that* too much?

In those one-on-one discussions with your attorney, be as specific as you want. Those conversations are privileged, so speak freely and honestly when it's just you and your lawyer. It is perfectly fine to brainstorm together how much (or how little) to seek from the court.

We would caution you, though, about allowing emotion to lead you into too drastic a request. Fairness and reason must prevail in these situations. For example, you may have a child that, for not the best of reasons, doesn't want to go visit your ex and nothing would make you happier than if the visitation didn't take place at all. So, instead of taking steps to address the underlying issues, you tell your lawyer you want to ask the court to eliminate your ex's visitation schedule (your ex's court-ordered access and possession rights), or at minimum, greatly restrict and reduce them. However, being too drastic in the relief you seek from the court can backfire in dramatic and unexpected ways. The court could come to the conclusion that you are not the best conservator to promote a relationship with the other parent. Seeing that you already have a solid relationship with the child, and given that the goal of the court is to place children in a position where they have the optimum relationship with *both* parents, taking such a drastic position could lead to the unintended, unexpected consequence of actually losing primary custody of the child. Again, your attorney will caution you against going too far in your requests to the court, so listen to them. And, frankly, if a client refuses to back down from unreasonable demands like this, their attorney may simply refuse to take the case.

All these things are fair game in your private conversations with your attorney. When it comes to drawing up the pleading, though, you need to step back from the specifics you've been discussing and understand that your lawyer will likely be as general as possible in the papers. The primary exception would be if you are seeking extraordinary relief, and the law requires you to include specific allegations in order to attain that relief. Your lawyer can always amend your pleading, but once you've gone on the record asking for a certain modification, you very well might need to answer why you sought such relief in the first place.

Occasionally, an attorney will advise you to aim higher than you'd settle for, even in your pleadings . For example, let's say you want to modify your custody agreement so that you and your co-parent share 50/50 custody, meaning your child lives with you half the time and with the other parent half the time. There are situations when it might make sense to overshoot what you actually want. In this example, an attorney may advise you to request full custody, rather than 50/50. This can be part of your lawyer's strategy to put the other party on the defensive. Rather than risk you getting full custody, the other parent may gladly accept a 50/50 access schedule as a compromise.

Another danger in going too far in the relief you're seeking from the court is that you may trigger a countersuit that otherwise would not have been filed. The truth is, once you file papers and serve them on your ex, you are probably going to be countersued anyway. It's standard operating procedure for the respondent to file a countersuit against the petitioner in these cases. However, if you overreach in the modifications you request in your pleading, the other party may come back at you with equally harsh demands in a countersuit. For example, if you file a motion to limit your ex's access, they may file a countersuit seeking a change of primary custody. So, in a sense, the party who sets the modification case in motion has the power to set the tone for the whole litigation battle. If you are reasonable and genuinely seeking what's best for the children, the respondent will hopefully match your tone and reasonableness in their response. If you start throwing grenades right at the start, you should expect to have some thrown back at you.

In your grounds and relief/modification requests, you must also state your conviction that these changes are in the best interests of the child. The court doesn't care if you and your ex simply don't like each other, and they'll likely punish you with a not-so-favorable ruling if you try to weaponize the court just to get back at your former spouse. The laws that govern SAPCRs are laser-focused on the well-being of the children involved, and in all likelihood (and we should add *hopefully*), the judge will be equally laser-focused. If it is not crystal clear that the modifications you're seeking are in the child's best interests (not the parents' best interests), then you may unwittingly start down a road that leads somewhere you do not want to go.

Whatever relief you're requesting from the court—whether it is a revision to the possession order, an increase in child support, or anything else—be sure to ask your attorney to spell out for you in clear terms what the rules, laws, and guidelines are for that specific relief. If you're requesting a change in the possession order, for example, you need to know what criteria the court will use in considering your request and what the potential repercussions could be from you initiating this request. These things can differ from jurisdiction to jurisdiction.

One last thing that is typically added to the pleading is a request for the court to order the opposing party to pay some or all your legal fees. But don't get your hopes up. This *is* awarded occasionally under certain circumstances, but it is extremely rare. So, if you're taking your ex back to court, you should expect to pay all your attorney and associated fees yourself. And if you do somehow get awarded a judgment for your legal fees, keep in mind that you're getting a *judgment*, not a cash award. That is a huge difference, and you still might never see a penny of what is owed to you. You will have to file that judgment in the county where you will attempt to collect it, and if the other party does not pay, your only remedy is to is to seek collection efforts like any other creditor. The bottom line here is that you cannot and should not rely on having your attorney's fees paid by the other party in a modification suit. You'll still be on the hook for paying your lawyer and the associated legal expenses. If you get anything, it will be in the form of reimbursement, and it will almost certainly take a while.

6. PRAYER

Appropriately, your pleading will end with a *prayer*, but not the type of prayer you should be doing daily as you go through blended family litigation! The prayer in your pleading is simply a summary of the relief you are requesting and often includes a prayer for *general relief*, a catch-all request.

Dennis

Here is a funny anecdote from my days as a full-time attorney. I handled a case for the respondent in a lawsuit in which the petitioner was representing himself without a lawyer. He was obviously using some instructions for the pleading that he got online or from a book, and those instructions rightfully instructed him to end the pleading with a prayer. However, they must not have given him a good example of what they meant by *prayer*, because he took the instruction a bit too literally.

Instead of ending his pleading with a summary of the relief he was requesting, he ended it with, "And now, dear Lord, I pray for the relief I am requesting in this lawsuit, in the name of the Father, the Son, and the Holy Spirit, Amen."

—————————

To help you avoid that kind of embarrassing situation, we have inserted a sample pleading document at the end of this chapter. This is an actual pleading from a real custody modification lawsuit. Of course, some information has been tweaked or blacked out in the interests of privacy, but otherwise, this should be very similar to what you either have served to or received from the other party in your own litigation.

Execution Phase Step 3:
File the Lawsuit with the Court

Once your attorney has prepared the appropriate paperwork for the pleading, they will submit it to the court. There isn't much to this. In some jurisdictions, the pleading will be submitted on paper, but most jurisdictions now receive them electronically. You might think of it like filing your taxes: you provide all the information to your CPA, who then pulls out the relevant details, fills out the proper forms, and clicks a few buttons to submit everything electronically to the IRS. Swap out *lawyer* in place of CPA and *court of jurisdiction* in place of the IRS, and it's pretty much the same type of process.

You might be wondering how long it takes to go from hiring a lawyer to filing the papers with the court. That really depends on the jurisdiction you're in and, more importantly, if there are any urgent matters that might require a court-issued protective order to remove the children from a dangerous situation. In most cases and in a typical jurisdiction, you can have papers filed with the court within a week or so of retaining counsel. Of course, this could change based on your attorney's caseload and how quickly they can get around to finishing the paperwork. It could also change based on when you *want* to file the papers. There are occasions when you might want to hold off a week or a month, such as trying to time everything for when your child is with you, so they aren't around when your ex is served with the lawsuit.

If there *are* urgent matters that might require immediate action by the court, your attorney will probably seek an *ex parte* order when the case is filed but before the papers are served. *Ex parte* means "without the other party." Essentially this is a quick meeting between your attorney and the judge without the other party having any representation or even any knowledge of the discussion taking place. You would only need this if there were extreme circumstances that pose an imminent risk to the safety and well-being of your child. Reasons for an *ex parte* order might include finding out your ex has developed a drinking problem and regularly gets black-out drunk when your child is staying with them; having good reason to believe your child is being abused; or learning that your ex has a new partner living with them that you sincerely believe poses a risk to your child.

In these situations, when your lawyer files the papers with the court, he or she would seek an immediate meeting with the judge to present sworn affidavits testifying to the imminent danger to the child. The goal here is to get an *ex parte order* that overrides the prior custody order and ensures your child's safety until the matter can be fully explored and resolved in the course of the litigation.

Be forewarned: If you seek an *ex parte* order that changes the status quo, you better be sure you can back up the accusations you're making with facts and evidence. An *ex parte* order that seeks to immediately modify in some way the standing final order is a big deal. Judges do not like issuing such orders without giving both sides the opportunity to state their case. If a judge issues such an order without giving the other party a chance to be heard, and if the judge later finds out that you were stretching the truth or exaggerating the danger, you will get off to a bad start with the judge. You will lose some trust right off the bat, and that could cost you in the long run. Also, an *ex parte* order that changes the status quo will have a limited life such that the order will expire soon unless it is extended after a hearing where both parties can be heard on the issue.

It is not that unusual for the petitioner to seek and obtain *ex parte* orders in the form of injunctive relief that are intended to preserve or protect, not change, the status quo. Examples would be an order that prohibits a parent from: removing the child from the jurisdiction of the court or from the child's current school or day-care facility; disturbing the peace of the child or of the party to the suit; hiding the child from you; making disparaging remarks regarding you in the presence of the children; discussing any litigation concerning the children in their presence or within their earshot; or consuming alcohol or using any illegal drug within a specific number of hours before or during that parent's periods of access to or possession of the child.

In some jurisdictions, these types of "preserve and keep the peace" injunctions are standard and will be automatically granted upon request. If the court does indeed grant the injunctive relief, it should be noted that the other party is not bound by those orders until they receive actual notice of the orders, which typically doesn't occur until they are served with the papers that would include the order containing the injunctive relief. One important caveat, though: if the other party has retained an attorney and you or your lawyer are aware of this, that attorney must be notified and given a reasonable opportunity to appear when you are seeking your *ex parte* relief.

If all this seems a lot less dramatic than you'd expect (apart from the *ex parte* exception), you're right. Petitioners are often surprised by how clinical the process can be up to this point. Sure, there is a lot going on emotionally, but from a legal and process standpoint, it's all very cut and dried so far. It may feel overwhelming to you, but it's just another Tuesday for your attorney. They do this all the time. We don't say that flippantly, either. Part of what makes your lawyer so valuable is their experience and largely dispassionate perspective on your situation. Yes, they care about you and have a duty to protect your interests, but they also have the ability to look at everything at arm's length and prevent you from making a huge, emotion-driven mistake.

Throwing the First Punch

The great poet and philosopher Mike Tyson once said, "Everybody has a plan until they get punched in the mouth."[1] It's true in boxing, and it's true in family court.

Everything up to this point—hiring a lawyer, drawing up the papers, and filing the papers—is relatively easy because everything has been in your favor (assuming you're the petitioner). You've made all the decisions, you've had all the control, you've done all this in private, and you haven't experienced any pushback from anyone. You've probably had some emotional anguish about actually pulling the trigger on this litigation, but you've only had to fight *yourself* so far. Now, however, once the papers are filed with the court, you've got to brace yourself. By filing the papers, you are throwing the first punch, and your ex will almost certainly come back up swinging.

In the next chapter, we'll continue the Execution phase by unpacking the four steps that take place between filing the court papers and actually going to trial. That's where things really get messy because that is when the petitioner drops the bomb on the other party. This is also where the respondent *enters* the litigation which means the tension, pushback, and arguments are about to begin in earnest.

So, buckle your seatbelt. Things are about to get bumpy.

---

1. "Mike Tyson Explains One of His Most Famous Quotes," *Sun Sentinel* (blog), November 9, 2012, https://www.sun-sentinel.com/2012/11/09/mike-tyson-explains-one-of-his -most-famous-quotes-3/.

NO. xxxxx

IN THE INTEREST OF	§	IN THE DISTRICT COURT
	§	
▮▮▮	§	▮▮th JUDICIAL DISTRICT
	§	
A CHILD	§	▮▮▮▮▮▮ COUNTY, TEXAS

MOTION TO MODIFY PARENT-CHILD RELATIONSHIP

1.   *Discovery Level*

Discovery in this case is intended to be conducted under level 2 of rule 190 of the Texas Rules of Civil Procedure.

2.   *Parties and Order to Be Modified*

This suit to modify a prior order is brought by xxxxxx, Petitioner. Petitioner is the biological father of the child and has standing to bring this suit. The requested modification will be in the best interest of the child.

Respondent is xxxxxx.

The order to be modified is entitled Agreed Order in Suit to Modify Parent-Child Relationship and was rendered on xxxxxxx xx, 20xx.

3.   *Jurisdiction*

This Court has continuing, exclusive jurisdiction of this suit.

4.   *Child*

The following child is the subject of this suit:

        Name: xxxxxx
        Sex: Female
        Birth date: xx/xx/20xx
        County of residence: ▮▮▮▮

5.   *Parties Affected*

The following parties may be affected by this suit:

Name: xxxxxx

Relationship: biological mother of child

Process should be served.

6.   *Child's Property*

There has been no change of consequence in the status of the child's property since the prior order was rendered.

7.   *Protective Order Statement*

8.   *Modification of Conservatorship, Possession and Access*

The order to be modified is not based on a mediated or collaborative law settlement agreement. The circumstances of the child, a conservator, or other party affected by the order to be modified have materially and substantially changed since the date of rendition of the order to be modified.

Preceding the filing of this suit, Respondent has engaged in a history or pattern of abusive behavior that significantly and detrimentally effects the physical health and emotional development of the child.

Petitioner requests that the Court consider this conduct in appointing the Petitioner as sole managing conservator or the parties as joint managing conservators.

Petitioner requests that the terms and conditions for access to or possession of the child be modified to provide as follows: Appointing Petitioner sole managing conservator of the child and ordering Respondent be excluded from possession of, or access to the child.

There is a history or pattern of child abuse committed by Respondent. Petitioner requests the Court to deny Respondent access to the child.

Respondent may violate the Court's order relating to Respondent's possessory interest in the child. Petitioner requests the Court to order Respondent to execute a bond or deposit security in a reasonable amount, conditioned on Respondent's compliance with the Court's orders concerning possession of and access to the child.

The requested modification is in the best interest of the child.

9. *Request for Temporary Orders*

Petitioner requests the Court, after notice and hearing, to make temporary orders for the safety and welfare of the child, including but not limited to the following:

Denying Respondent access to the child or, alternatively, rendering a possession order providing that Respondent's periods of visitation be continuously supervised.

With regard to the requested temporary order for managing conservatorship, Petitioner would show the Court the following:

These temporary orders are necessary because the child's present circumstances would significantly impair the child's physical health or emotional development, and the requested temporary order is in the best interest of the child. See the affidavit of Petitioner attached as Exhibit A.

10. *Request for Temporary Restraining Order*

Petitioner requests the Court to dispense with the necessity of a bond, and Petitioner requests that Respondent be temporarily restrained immediately, without hearing, and after notice and hearing be temporarily enjoined, pending the further order of this Court, from:

Disturbing the peace of the child or of another party.

Withdrawing the child from enrollment in the school or day-care facility where the child is presently enrolled.

Hiding or secreting the child from Petitioner.

Making disparaging remarks regarding Petitioner in the presence or within the hearing of the child.

Discussing any litigation concerning the child in the presence or within the hearing of the child.

Consuming alcohol within the eight (8) hours before or during the period of possession of or access to the child.

As the basis for the extraordinary relief requested below, Petitioner would show that before the filing of this petition Respondent has engaged in the conduct stated in the affidavit attached as Exhibit A. Based on that affidavit, Petitioner requests the Court to grant the following relief:

Issue an order excluding Respondent from possession of or access to the child, xxxxxxr.

11. *Request for Attorney's Fees, Expenses, Costs, and Interest*

It was necessary for Petitioner to secure the services of xxxxxxx, a licensed attorney, to preserve and protect the child's rights. Respondent should be ordered to pay reasonable attorney's fees, expenses, and costs through trial and appeal, and a judgment should be rendered in favor of this attorney and against Respondent and be ordered paid directly to Petitioner's attorney, who may enforce the judgment in the attorney's own name. Petitioner requests postjudgment interest as allowed by law.

12. *Prayer*

Petitioner prays that citation and notice issue as required by law and that the Court enter its orders in accordance with the allegations contained in this petition.

Petitioner prays that the Court immediately grant a temporary restraining order restraining Respondent, in conformity with the allegations of this petition, from the acts set forth above, and Petitioner prays that, after notice and hearing, this temporary restraining order be made a temporary injunction.

Petitioner prays for attorney's fees, expenses, costs, and interest as requested above.

Petitioner prays for general relief.

Respectfully submitted,

Law Offices xx xxxx xxxxxx
xxxx x xxxx xx.
xxxx, xxxx xxxxx
(xxx) xxx-xxxx
(xxx) xxx-xxxx Fax

By:_____
xxxx x xxxxx
State Bar No. xxxxxxxx
xxxxxxxxx@xxxxxxxxx.com
Attorney for Petitioner

CERTIFICATE OF SERVICE

I certify that a true copy of this Motion to Modify Parent-Child Relationship was served in accordance with rule 21a of the Texas Rules of Civil Procedure on the following on ____20xx:

xxxxx by electronic filing manager.

xxxx x. xxxxxx
Attorney for xxxxx xxxxxx

CERTIFICATE OF CONFERENCE

I, xxxx xxxxxx, attorney for xxxxxxx, hereby certify as follows:

Prior to presenting this matter to a Judge for approval, I contacted all attorneys of record, transmitted a copy of the pleadings and proposed order in this matter, and notified them that I was requesting such ex parte relief, and we were unable to reach an agreement, at which time I notified all attorneys of record that I would present this matter to the Court at 9:00 a.m. on xxxxxxx xx, xxxx in the 325th District Court and invited them to attend prior to signing.

_____
XXXX X. XXXXXXX
Attorney for Petitioner

Chapter 6

DROPPING THE BOMB

Well, here we are. Papers have been drawn up and filed with the court. Any day now, *someone* is going to get a knock at the door. And that knock is going to change everyone's lives. Whether you're the petitioner or the respondent, your life is going to be stressful and busy for the next several months (unless you settle the case early, which can happen at any time in the process). You're going to have hard conversations. You might be accused of some terrible things. Your children are going to be stuck in the middle of a tense situation. It's a wild rollercoaster of emotions and legal proceedings, but at this point, it's a ride you *are* going on. So let's continue the discussion of the Execution phase by exploring what happens after the papers are delivered and before you get to court.

Stages of a Typical Modification Case

1. Petitioner (the one initiating the lawsuit) hires a lawyer.

2. Petitioner draws up lawsuit papers.

3. Petitioner files the lawsuit with the court.

4. Petitioner has the papers served.

5. Respondent answers the suit.

6. Pre-trial motions and hearings.

7. Discovery process.

8. Negotiation.

9. Trial preparation.

10. Trial proceedings.

11. Rendition (the judge or jury renders a verdict).

12. Final order drawn up by the attorneys and signed by the judge.

13. Appeal process.

You are here

Execution Phase Step 4: Serve the Papers

Once the papers are drawn up and filed with the court, the next step is for those papers to be delivered—usually *hand-delivered*—to the respondent. This is when things get real. Up to this point, the petitioner has been working behind the scenes, getting their ducks in a row, and making plans without any pushback or controversy. But now, the word is out. By serving the papers, the petitioner is letting the respondent know that their life is about to change. At the very least, their life is about to get extremely stressful and complicated for a while, so do not take this action for granted, regardless of which side of the lawsuit you're on.

Because the act of serving the papers is essentially the "shot across the bow" of the respondent, how the petitioner serves the papers can set the tone for the entire process. If you have it done privately and professionally, perhaps even scheduling the delivery of the papers by phone instead of having the process server show up unannounced, you'll communicate that you want to handle the matter respectfully. If, however, you have the server deliver the papers in the middle of your child's soccer game, while the respondent is trying to cheer the child on and surrounded by other parents, you'll communicate something else. That is how these cases start off on the wrong foot. Nastiness contaminates the case from the moment the papers are delivered. Every step of the Execution phase is an opportunity to communicate *something* to the other party, and that begins with the delivery of the papers.

But let's back up a bit. *Serving the papers* simply means physically getting the pleading into the hands of the respondent. This notice advises the respondent that a lawsuit has been filed and informs them that they have a certain amount of time to respond to the lawsuit.

The most common way of serving a lawsuit is to have the papers served by a *private process server*. This is someone who is hired by the petitioner's attorney to hand-deliver the pleading to the responding party. While it seems pretty straightforward, the process server cannot be any random courier off the street. Rather, this person must have the government-sponsored authority to serve legal pleadings in that specific jurisdiction. And, of course, because this server is engaged by and working for the petitioner's attorney, the cost is passed back to the petitioner. So, if you're having papers served, you're paying for it.

Scott

Papers are usually served within a week or so of being filed with the court. Because there is this slight delay between the petitioner *filing* the papers and the respondent *receiving* the papers, it's possible the respondent may find out something is coming before the papers are served. For example, I was once involved in a business-related lawsuit (not family court) several years ago. I had no idea it was coming until I started getting a lot of phone calls and mailers from different lawyers one week. Apparently, every lawyer in my area knew this lawsuit was coming before I did! Once the papers were filed with the court, all these attorneys started jockeying for my business. After noticing this strange flood of legal eagles appearing out of nowhere, I finally received the actual lawsuit at my door. Suddenly, all those marketing calls made sense.

ETIQUETTE IN SERVING PAPERS

If you are the petitioner, and especially if the respondent does not know the lawsuit is coming, remember that this is, in effect, you throwing the first punch. No matter how politely you try to do it, you'll still be dropping a bomb in the middle of your ex's life, and that act has consequences. How you go about this action will largely communicate the tone for how you will behave throughout the litigation. This is crucial to keep in mind since both parties must continue co-parenting together throughout the litigation and long after it's over. However, you can at least try to mitigate the damage and backlash by following some basic etiquette in serving the papers. Your goal here should not be to bring unnecessary harm or embarrassment but to simply get the ball rolling.

Papers are usually served within a week in most cases, unless the server has a hard time finding the respondent (which we'll discuss below). Because the process server works for your lawyer (if you're the petitioner and you're using a private process server), you have a lot of control over when, where, and how the papers are served. (That is, of course, unless you are in a jurisdiction where the lawsuit is typically served by a county employee such as a constable.) For example, you can ask them to avoid serving the papers in public if possible, and you can request a particular day when you know your child won't be present. Or, if the server cannot find the respondent, you can provide some insight on when and where to locate them.

In some cases, the process server may make a phone call to arrange a specific time and place with the respondent before attempting to deliver the papers. This is especially helpful if you want to avoid any embarrassment or chance of the respondent being served in public. Similarly, if the respondent already has an attorney in place, your attorney can call the other party's attorney to let them know something is coming and ask if the opposing attorney wants to accept service on behalf of their client.

Tips for the Respondent Upon Getting Served

Now, let's switch roles and assume you are the respondent. Being handed a lawsuit—especially if it comes with no warning—is a terrifying and stressful ordeal. How is someone supposed to keep a level head when their former partner is dragging them into court and challenging their parental rights?

Start by giving yourself some grace. You aren't going to do everything right. You will make mistakes. No one has ever had a "perfect" family court litigation experience, and you almost certainly will not be the first. That said, there are several suggestions we've collected from our years of experience working with many families in litigation. If you don't do anything else, please try to follow these six tips if you are served legal papers:

1. Do not avoid the process server.

There is no point in hiding from the process server or actively trying to make it more difficult for them to do their job. At this point, the lawsuit is *going* to happen. Avoiding the server does nothing to help you or your case. In fact, if you avoid it long enough, it could lead to the petitioner seeking an order from the court for *substituted service*, in which case the court could find that you will (theoretically) receive sufficient notice if the papers are left at your doorstep. This substituted service might give you less actual notice (time to respond) than if you had simply accepted service initially. Plus, the petitioner has incurred additional fees and expenses that could be assessed against you. Worse, the court is advised, without you being present, that you have evaded service. Also, trying to avoid the process server greatly increases your chances of having it done in a very public, embarrassing manner. Most servers would prefer to hand you the papers privately at your front door or at a pre-arranged meeting place. They will, however, serve you at work, at a school event, at your child's baseball game, at a public picnic, or anywhere else they can find you. The bottom line is that you are going to be served one way or another. This is not a situation in which you can avoid the problem until it simply goes away. It won't. It will only get worse the longer you avoid it. If you know you are about to be served and you have an attorney, they will know how to get a copy of the lawsuit even before you are served. So, if you have a lawyer already, let them know a process server is trying to serve you. If you are concerned you will be served with papers that could have *ex parte* orders that go into effect when you are served or that have a limited response time from date of service, let a lawyer direct you on what to do.

2. Take a breath.

You don't have to respond immediately. Take a day to let it sink in. Don't rush into anything or fire off a response to the other party that you might regret later. You do not want to make a rash decision that is going to ultimately hurt your situation even more by trying to punish the other parent. Yes, you have some work to do, and you will need to find a lawyer quickly to help you draft your response by the deadline given in the papers. But that won't happen today. You just took a hit; take a moment to catch your breath before you come up swinging.

3. Remind yourself that nothing is changing today.

The prior orders (from either your divorce or a previous modification) remain in effect until they are updated or replaced with new final court orders. The exception, as we've mentioned, would be if there are *ex parte* or temporary orders that come into play during the pendency of the suit. Nonetheless, you are still parenting with the person who is suing you, and you are still responsible for everything else covered in your existing orders that are not temporarily altered by an *ex parte* order or a subsequent temporary order. You may be angry about the lawsuit, but you must still honor the controlling custody and parent-child provisions.

4. Guard your words carefully from this point on.

As we've said several times, you will be parenting under a microscope throughout this litigation. Anything you do or say now will be heavily scrutinized. Assume anything you say to the other party will come back to haunt you when it is read back to you by an attorney at some point during the litigation process. And, of course, the social media guidelines we discussed in Chapter 4 should be in full effect.

5. Get small.

We often advise people to "get small" during a litigation. That is, you want to form a very small circle around yourself and be judicious in what you say and to whom you say it from this point on. Even if you have a big, outgoing, life-of-the-party personality, we suggest shrinking your world as you go through your lawsuit. As we've said before, anything you do or say—especially during the pendency of your case—can and likely will be brought into the litigation. Do not give the other party any extra ammunition they could use against you.

6. *Keep the kids out of it.*

We addressed this at length in Chapter 4, but it bears repeating here: leave the kids out of it. Let your children be children. Do not vent to them or look to them for your emotional support. If your children are very young, it is best to not say anything at all. If they are teenagers, you might just say that you and the other parent are in the process of discussing and possibly changing some things and that you're getting help from some professionals to sort it out. Of course, the other parent may not follow this advice and might try to bring the children into it. If your kids come home from visiting the other parent and ask about the lawsuit, do not take that as permission to spill your guts to them. Keep it to a bare minimum and speak respectfully about the other parent (or don't say anything at all about them).

Execution Phase Step 5: Answer the Suit

The papers that are served give the respondent a deadline for responding. Three weeks or so is typical in most states. In Texas, where we live, it is usually worded as, "by 10:00 am on the Monday next following the expiration of twenty days after (the date you were served)." That's legalese for, "You must reply by 10:00 am on the Monday following twenty days from today." The clock starts for your reply when the papers are delivered, not when the case is filed with the court. So again, if you've been served, you have *some* time; you just don't have a *lot* of time.

If the lawsuit comes as a surprise and you do not have an attorney yet, that means you must start acting quickly to find the best attorney for your case. You will need that attorney to help you respond to the suit, so don't waste any time. Try to retain a lawyer within a week of being served so that you have time to get them up to speed on your situation, prepare your response, and file it by the deadline.

In the previous chapter, we described the initial pleading as a legal form that states the petitioner's grounds for change and requested remedies. The respondent's official reply, usually called the *respondent's original answer*, is similar. It's a simple form that is filed with the court that states your intent to actively participate in the case. In legal-speak, it *puts into issue* what has been alleged in the lawsuit. This is important, because once this document is filed with the court, you and your attorney are immediately entitled to receive notice of any proceedings that are scheduled from that point forward. That may seem obvious, but remember what we said in the previous chapter about *ex parte* hearings, or meetings the petitioner's lawyer may have had with the judge without the respondent's participation or knowledge. Once you file an answer to the suit, you won't need to worry about that. Your lawyer will be made aware of *any* action sought or taken on your case.

If you've been served papers and you disagree with the change being sought by the petitioner, you would file what's commonly called a *general denial* with the court. This is the family civil court version of a *not guilty* plea. This puts the case into issue and prevents the judge from entering a decision without you having an opportunity to appear to either agree or contest the matter.

You may be thinking, *What are the chances that I WOULDN'T contest the matter?!*

That's understandable, especially if you've just been slapped with a lawsuit out of the blue. After all, the term *lawsuit* carries all kinds of negative connotations. However, not all lawsuits are contested or even that big of a deal. There are situations, in fact, when two parties openly and willingly enter a lawsuit in order to make adjustments to the custody and/or support order that they previously agreed to.

A lawsuit is a necessary step in having the court officially change a prior decree. Often, two parties work together without litigation to decide on changes they both agree would be best for the child. However, those changes cannot be enforced by the court unless they are officially rendered by a judge and reflected in new orders to replace or amend the existing orders. Even though each parent is agreeable to the change in this situation, they can't simply ask the court to update the existing order. That can only be done in the context of a lawsuit. So, in that situation, as strange as it may sound, one party would need to file a lawsuit against the other. That's the only way to get this matter before the court. In these cases, the respondent may have no objection to what is being alleged in the pleading and can then have their attorney answer the lawsuit with an affirmative statement reflecting their agreement to the proposed changes. The petitioner can state in the initiating suit that they believe the parties will agree on the requested change(s). In this situation, you might not need to officially serve the respondent with the pleading. Instead, the respondent can sign off on a proposed agreed order to be presented to the court. If the papers *are* formally served, though, it's best to file a simple answer. That way, if things fall apart later, the respondent will still be entitled to notice before any action is taken.

Similarly, a lawsuit might be used to codify changes you and your ex have *already* made unofficially. For example, the prior orders may say that the mother has the right to establish the children's primary domicile or has primary custody, and the father gets the child every other weekend. But maybe for the past couple of years, everyone has got into the habit of the child alternating between living with Mom for a week and then living with Dad for a week, making it more of a 50/50 custody situation in practice, even though that's not what was outlined in the official order. Everyone may be perfectly fine and comfortable with this arrangement, but Dad could always have this concern in the back of his mind that if he makes any mistake or misstep, Mom can pull them back to the letter of the law and the standing order.

In this situation, Dad may simply seek to have the orders changed to reflect what they have already been doing anyway. That way, he doesn't have to worry about Mom suddenly yanking back his alternating weeks with his kids. Ideally, he would discuss this with Mom, and they could mutually agree to change the orders by having him initiate a lawsuit and having her answer acknowledging that she believes the parties will present a proposed agreed order for the court to approve and enter.

Other times, you may not already have a new agreement on modifications, but you are also not that opposed to what the other party is requesting. When faced with the expense, stress, and drama of a full-blown, hard-fought lawsuit, you might review the pleading and say, "Okay, this is what they're requesting. Do I want to fight this? Does this seem reasonable? Would simply agreeing to these changes from the start be in the best interest of my child? Is this a resolution I can live with?" It may be a bitter pill to swallow, and it may take a few days to get there, but take an honest look at the situation and decide if what the other party is asking for is worth putting yourself and your children through a prolonged litigation experience.

If you've been served papers you were not expecting and do not agree with, though, you'll need to file an answer indicating your intent to fight the allegations and relief outlined in the pleading. At this point, this case officially becomes a two-horse race.

Execution Phase Step 6: Pre-Trial Motions and Hearings

In the previous chapter, we talked about urgent, immediate, *ex parte* conferences an attorney might have with the judge when the suit is filed. That process represents a type of *pre-trial motion and hearing*. As we have said, those are usually held when there is an imminent threat or danger to the child's well-being, such as if the respondent is potentially abusive or dealing with a substance abuse problem. But there are other types of pre-trial motions and hearings that may come into play as soon as the papers have been served.

You would seek a temporary hearing with a pre-trial motion if you believed it was necessary to put temporary orders in place to replace the prior court orders for the duration of the litigation (the *pendency* of the suit). Remember, no matter how long the litigation process takes, both parties are obligated to maintain the existing custody orders for the duration of the case. However, there are some situations in which the court would need to take more immediate action with a temporary order. This provides an immediate (but temporary) change to your existing orders to get you through the trial, when your new final orders are granted.

Pre-trial motions and hearings dealing with substantive issues (concerning custody and parent-child issues) are typically designed for matters that are *time-sensitive* but not *emergency* situations. But because court dockets are usually so full, you might be waiting awhile for a temporary hearing. Also, you might be given a very limited amount of time to present your case for temporary orders. This can be a challenge, because you must make your case with what might be very little concrete evidence, and you or your attorney might have to shoot from the hip a bit because you've not yet been through the discovery process (which we'll discuss next). Making it even tougher is the fact that the judge may only give you a twenty-minute hearing to deal with the issue.

Many people try to jump into a pre-trial motion for temporary orders because they want an immediate change without ever considering whether that action is necessary. That is a big mistake for at least four reasons: First, if you do not have a compelling reason to request an immediate change to your existing orders, you'll likely have your motion denied. Second, you will have presented your case half-cocked and maybe not present nearly as compelling of an argument as you could have after completing discovery. That could work against you in the long run. Third, pre-trial hearings add a significant new expense to your overall case, because you are essentially adding a mini-trial to your ongoing litigation, which translates to more attorney's fees. Fourth, if your motion is denied, you will have likely lost some ground psychologically in the negotiation game that is always in play and possibly strategically by giving the opposing party an early win.

For these reasons, we recommend using substantive pre-trial motions sparingly. They are *substantive* in the sense that they deal with parent-child issues as opposed to *procedural* pre-trial issues that your attorney might pursue, such as if you are seeking to expand or limit certain discovery tools. The pre-trial hearings we are discussing here are different as well from certain pre-trial hearings the court might actually require, such as, setting ground rules for discovery, scheduling a final trial setting, setting time limits, requiring each party to submit a witness list, and so on.

Substantive pre-trial motions should only be used if absolutely necessary and only if your attorney believes the issue is worth addressing sooner rather than later and that you have a decent shot at getting the temporary orders you're seeking. Examples of when this kind of urgent action would be reasonable include situations when one parent:

- Needs to move.
- Wants to make a school-related change, such as changing schools or switching to homeschool.
- Is suggesting that the child himself or herself wants to come live with them and wants that change to happen immediately.
- Wants to bring in a mediator, parent facilitator, or parent coordinator and the other party is resistant. In this situation, a judge could order the family to seek a resolution using those resources. This has the additional benefit of making the person requesting mediation look reasonable in the eyes of the court. It shows the court that you are actively trying to resolve the matter, but the other party is resistant.
- Is actively violating the prior orders. For example, if a parent is trying to withhold visitation from the other parent, you might need the judge to step in and force compliance or add some provisions that enforce the current decree.

Execution Phase Step 7: Discovery

Discovery is the process of gathering potentially relevant information and evidence for the case, either voluntarily or compulsorily, from all parties. This is by far the longest, most difficult, and most maddening part of the litigation process. It can also be the most expensive part. Even those who enter litigation passionate and energized about their case can and will lose steam before they're out of the discovery phase, especially if your case involves a high-stakes custody battle. It takes a huge toll mentally, spiritually, emotionally, and physically. We don't want to scare you, but to be honest, the discovery phase can be very *hard*.

With that trigger warning, let's dig into what happens during a thorough trial discovery. Your lawyer's chief goal in discovery is to gather, organize, and categorize everything that is or could be relevant to your case. And we do mean *everything*. This includes several different actions and types of information, including:

REQUIRED DISCLOSURES

Some jurisdictions—Texas courts, for example—require parties in a lawsuit to automatically provide certain information soon after the initiation of the suit and before a trial. You will be ahead of the game if you followed our advice in Chapter 4 about getting things together for your attorney. Examples of the type of information that may be required for automatic disclosure to the other party are: the factual basis of the party's claims or defenses; the name, address, and telephone number of persons having knowledge of relevant facts and a brief statement about their connection to the case; a list of potential witnesses and explanation of their connection to the case; and information regarding experts (psychologists, counselors, medical doctors, etc.) that a party might choose to call as expert witnesses. It is important to comply with the applicable disclosures required by a court, because failure to do so can result in sanctions including the exclusion of evidence that would otherwise be admissible—even evidence that could be critical to a party's case.

WRITTEN INTERROGATORIES

This is a list of questions an attorney can send to a party that require clear, written responses. Interrogatories are usually a party's first insight into how arduous this process is going to be, because a good attorney will send a barrage of questions. There are some limits on the number of questions the lawyer can send, but it is certainly enough to keep someone busy and more than a little intimidated. You should start out assuming that you are going to have to answer every question that is asked, but you can also depend on your lawyer to not only know to what extent you need to respond but also if there are legitimate objections to some of the questions.

REQUEST FOR PRODUCTION OF DOCUMENTS

This is essentially a laundry list of items that a party has been requested to produce. There's some overlap between a request for production of documents and what is asked in written interrogatories. Fair warning: this will keep you up at night looking through boxes of documents and photographs in the attic and going back through years' worth of emails! As is the case with other forms of discovery, if you fail to produce a requested document, you could find yourself unable to use the document or the information that could be derived from the document at trial. You could also be sanctioned by the court, requiring you to pay the fees and expenses incurred by your ex in compelling you to properly respond to their discovery requests.

REQUEST FOR ADMISSIONS

This is a process in which a party is given a statement and required to either admit or deny it while under oath. Failure to timely respond can lead to the statements being deemed true as a matter of law—a dangerous trap for the unwary!

DEPOSITIONS

This is by far the most intimidating part of the discovery phase for most people. It is a big enough deal that we need to slow down here and discuss depositions in detail.

Depositions 101

A deposition is a proceeding in which a person, the *deponent*, is questioned under oath in the presence of a stenographer who records everything that's said, except for any instances in which the attorneys agree to go off the record. The deposition may, with proper notice, be video recorded as well. If your deposition is taken (it's not automatic), your ex's attorney will put forth questions that you are required to answer verbally, under oath, and in the presence of a stenographer who records what is said.

You do not know the questions beforehand, and the opposing attorney questions you just like they do in court, using all their crafty little tricks to pull out the information they're looking for. This alone can make a deposition an incredibly intimidating experience, but that anxiety is compounded by the fact that this is often the first time the two parties will be in the same room since the lawsuit started. That's right—your ex will be staring at you as you answer their lawyer's questions. This can be extraordinarily nerve-racking—especially if you've spent the past several weeks or months avoiding this person, arguing over the phone with them (not recommended), or, worse, bad-mouthing them to anyone who would listen (definitely not recommended). Then, after all that, you're suddenly sitting across from them in a small room answering difficult questions about yourself, your ex, your current marriage, your children, and your life since the last order was entered. You might also be required to answer questions that, under various exceptions in the rules of evidence, allow opposing counsel to delve back into matters that occurred before the last order was entered. These are *not* fun days for anyone.

The deposition will usually take place in one of the attorneys' offices or conference rooms—possibly in the office of the lawyer who's asking the questions. By this point in the case, you have probably been to your attorney's office several times. There's a certain level of comfort there because you know they are fighting for you. However, when you go to the opposing attorney's office, you understand that this person and everyone in that office is working *against* you. It is intimidating to realize you are doing battle in enemy territory.

There is also intimidation in the fact that you are having to divulge so much private information to a handful of strangers. And in these cases, the information can be the most private and intimate facts of your life. Generally, a deposition would include both parties, attorneys for both parties, a court reporter, possibly a videographer, and possibly associate attorneys or paralegals—and everyone's eyes will be on you the whole time you're talking. Smirks, smiles, raised voices, stare downs, and long pauses don't get recorded unless the deposition is videotaped (one of several reasons a party might go to the extra expense of videoing the deposition—and likewise a reason someone might *not* want to videotape the deposition). However, the opposing counsel might verbally note a facial expression or shift in your body language, which then puts it in the transcript and on the record.

A typical deposition takes several hours. In some cases, though, a deposition could last all day or through multiple meetings over a couple of days. There can be some time limitations imposed on depositions by the court, but it is rare for the parties themselves to bump up against that limit. If the attorneys think they need more time than the court-approved limit, they can move the court for more time (which may or may not be granted). It is more likely that extra time would be allowed to thoroughly depose the parties and/or an expert witness (such as a mental health professional who must qualify as an expert in order to give opinion testimony). Time limits and the pocketbook force the attorneys to keep an eye on the clock and possibly adjust their game plan for who they depose and how much they spend deposing each nonparty as well as the opposing party. Don't expect your attorney to ask you questions during your deposition. It is allowed, but generally your attorney never does so unless you said something your attorney thinks needs to be cleared up or explained on the spot in the deposition and cannot wait to be clarified or explained at trial.

Dennis

The Attorney's Job in a Deposition

Let me say a word about objections in a deposition. Remember, at a deposition there is no judge present to rule on objections as there is when you are in trial. Also, different rules of evidence apply in a deposition. This is discovery, and as such, the attorneys are allowed to go beyond *relevancy*. The objection of *irrelevant* to a question posed might be a valid objection at trial and might very well be sustained by the judge, but it's not a valid objection in a deposition where the questions are allowed to explore matters that might lead to relevant facts. If a question goes beyond that standard, it could be proper for your attorney to instruct you not to answer, but know that will not go well for your attorney or for you if the question was proper and opposing counsel takes the matter up later in a motion for sanctions for failure to properly respond to discovery.

Judges hate gamesmanship in discovery, but also there are fine lines between gamesmanship and rightfully protecting one's client. The lines are fuzzy, and different judges can draw the lines differently—another reason it is helpful to be familiar with your judge and his or her tendencies. Penalties for crossing these lines can include attorney's fees being awarded against your attorney or you and, in some cases, testimony you need in court could be disallowed if your judge determines your side was not playing by the rules and wasting the court's time and the other party's time and expenses. These are matters your attorney must manage, and you must follow your attorney's lead here.

One more thing about objections in a deposition: Often, an objection will be made to the *form* of a question that could lead your attorney to instruct you not to answer until the question is rephrased and, for example, no longer assumes *facts not in evidence*. The often-cited example of a question that assumes *facts not in evidence* is, "When did you stop beating your wife?" As you can see, the *form*, or phrasing, of the question assumes abuse was taking place. Another common objection would be if the questioning attorney combines two questions into a single question.

Your attorney can make other objections to a question asked in a deposition for later rulings by the court, but you are still required to answer the question in the moment. Don't let this befuddle you; pause, let the process take place, and proceed as your attorney directs. There is a lot going into all this, "to object or not to object," "to instruct your client to answer or not," "to object to questions for the record." This is what you pay your attorney to effectively and knowledgably handle, so let your lawyer deal with it and avoid getting caught up in it or distracted by it.

Now, with that said, let me explain what I, as an attorney, am doing during the deposition. Whenever I'm deposing a witness—especially the opposing party to a case—I'm focused on doing three things. You should assume the lawyer asking the questions in your deposition is doing these things too. First, I want to lock the person into sworn testimony. Remember, you give a deposition *under oath*—the same oath you'd take on the witness stand at trial. You are required to answer the questions fully and honestly (unless your attorney has instructed you not to answer, as discussed above). So, when I have someone in court and ask the same question I asked them earlier in depositions, I already know the answer. If what the person says in court does not match what they said in the deposition, I will pull out their deposition transcript (I already have the page number and lines noted in my question outline), ask permission from the judge to approach the witness, and have them read aloud what they previously said in their sworn deposition. If what they said *then* doesn't match what they're saying *now*, it will be obvious that I've caught them in a lie—a lie they told under oath. Not surprisingly, judges and juries don't like that.

Also, in a custody case, I will typically seek to have the opposing party state positive facts about my client. I can either get them to help me paint a positive picture of my client, at least in part, or on the other hand, if they can't say one good thing about the person they chose to marry and co-parent with, well, that might be even more helpful to my case. One way or the other, I have them locked into a lot of testimony about my client and can prepare accordingly for when we are in trial.

Second, I'm trying to learn the facts of the case. As I ask my questions, I'm thinking, *What are you going to say as to the elements I must prove at trial? What are you going to say about yourself? What are the differences between what you say versus what my client has told me? What can I prove? Which of your claims can I poke holes in?* Sometimes, it will become obvious that my client hasn't told me the full story (which always only hurts the case). In those situations, I know I need to sit down with my client and root out all the information I need to do my job for them. Other times, it becomes obvious that they are misrepresenting what I know to be true about my client or a specific interaction, so I can dig into that in order to impeach their credibility later. And, of course, sometimes what they say matches exactly what I was expecting, and it's clear that both parties are at least honestly trying to get to the best outcome for their child.

Third, I'm often trying to make the deposition process as painful as possible for the opposing party. Don't take this the wrong way. A good attorney will use the deposition to force the opposing party to think about whether they really want to take this case all the way to trial. If I think it is not in my client's best interest to go to trial for any reason (financial burden, emotional toll, my client may not be a great witness, etc.), I'm going make the deposition a little extra painful for the opposing party. This is one way I can try to steer them toward mediation and settlement, which is almost always a better option than going all the way to trial.

The important takeaway for you here is that you must assume the opposing attorney who is deposing you is doing exactly the same things I do when I'm questioning someone. This is something you need to keep in mind as you head into your own deposition.

Scott

Your Job in a Deposition

Dennis told you what the questioning attorney's job is during a deposition. Now, let's focus on what *you* should be doing when you're giving your deposition.

First, be respectful to everyone at all times. You are going to get frustrated. You are going to get irritated with the lawyer asking you questions. You are going to be annoyed sitting across from your ex. That's fine. You can *be* frustrated, irritated, and annoyed; you just cannot *act* frustrated, irritated, and annoyed. Do whatever it takes to be respectful and polite. We'll talk more about this in the next chapter as it relates to the trial, but it applies here too.

Second, your whole demeanor during your deposition should follow what I call the James 1:19 Rule, "My dear brothers and sisters, take note of this: *Everyone should be quick to listen, slow to speak and slow to become angry*" (James 1:19 NIV, emphasis added). That's good advice pretty much anytime, but it's *especially* good advice when you are giving a deposition. Let's break down James's counsel piece by piece:

1. **Be quick to listen:** Listen carefully to the question being asked and *only* answer the question being asked. Do not volunteer any additional information beyond the straight (and honest) answer to the question. If the question is unclear or vague or you don't think it is specific enough, ask for clarification before you start answering.

2. **Be slow to speak:** Don't jump into an answer. Let each question hang in the air for a second or two. This gives you time to make sure you understand the exact question being asked and tailor your answer to those boundaries. Plus, this gives your attorney time to object if they think the question is inappropriate for any reason.

3. **Be slow to become angry:** Do not get emotional or overreact to a question or the lawyer's response to your answer. If a lawyer sees that they can easily get under your skin, they're going to do it a lot more. This also shows them that they could really "play" you if they got you on the stand in a trial. Under questioning, you will almost certainly get worked up and defensive, and you might naturally start saying things to defend yourself or explain your position. Usually what is said at this point is beyond the scope of the question. This is always a mistake. The most damaging testimony you could give is often an answer you never *had* to give. If you feel like you are on the verge of having an outburst, ask to take a break.

Third, do not refer to notes when answering questions. You might want to bring notes with you so you can answer more precisely and to help prevent nerves from making you forget things. That's a bad idea for a reason you probably wouldn't expect: if you refer to notes while answering the lawyer's questions, that lawyer has the right to ask to see whatever you are looking at. That means all your detailed notes could be brought into evidence. In effect, you could end up answering a lot of questions that no one was going to ask you. This is true even if you are reading notes on your phone or another device. The best rule of thumb is to not bring anything into the deposition that your attorney doesn't know about. And if you and your attorney decide that a few notes are okay to bring, expect the opposing attorney to ask for them.

Fourth, say, "I don't recall" whenever necessary. There's no problem in saying this unless you start saying it for every question. If you genuinely do not remember the details around what the attorney is asking you, just tell them you do not recall. Do not sit there and try to make up an answer or start rambling in an attempt to create an answer or to stall for time while you try to come up with the answer. All that unnecessary nervous chatter could get you in a lot of trouble, and it is all being recorded by the stenographer.

Fifth, take breaks when necessary. You are free to ask for a break when you need one, either for a bathroom break, a mental break, or to confer with your attorney. You don't need to give a reason; just say you need a quick break. If you overuse breaks, however, you could give the impression that you are trying to confer with your attorney for every question. The opposing attorney can ask you about that when you reconvene to make sure it is on the record. They can't properly ask you what you discussed with your attorney, which is privileged, but they can make an issue out of every time you took a break to talk to your attorney. They could then try to use this to impeach your credibility, alleging that you are unable or unwilling to answer questions without checking everything with your attorney or taking time to think through how to best craft your answer. It is like pleading the Fifth Amendment: it is perfectly legal, but it can also give a certain unfavorable impression to the other side.

Sixth, do not allow yourself to be lulled into a false sense of security. The opposing attorney may be extremely polite and nice to you. Of course, it may be genuine, but you should assume it is a tactic. They want you to feel comfortable. They want you to feel like they are your friend. They want you to relax your defenses a bit so that they can get you to say things you would not have otherwise said.

But the opposing attorney is not your friend. They are not working for you, and they are not focused on your best interests. Be respectful and answer honestly but keep your guard up and stay on your toes.

Seventh, do not let your mind wander. It's natural to let your mind wander during long presentations or conversations, especially if you struggle with ADHD. You cannot afford to let this happen during a deposition. A deposition is mentally taxing. If you find yourself getting tired or unable to keep up, ask for a break. Do not risk saying anything you didn't mean to say just because your brain is fried.

Eighth and last, always—*always*—tell the truth. If you're caught saying one thing in a deposition and another thing on the witness stand at trial, you are busted. Everything in a deposition is done under oath. If you're caught lying, you will immediately be seen as untrustworthy, and your *entire* testimony can be suspect. That is a terrible position to be in. As we said in Chapter 3, always be honest with your attorney, and always be honest in answering questions under oath. You don't need to volunteer information the opposing attorney didn't ask for, but you must honestly answer the questions they do ask (unless your lawyer objects and instructs you not to answer as we've discussed).

———————

Your Job While the Other Party is Being Deposed

Clearly, you've got to keep your head in the game while you are facing the opposing attorney's questions in a deposition—but that's not the *only* deposition you must deal with. You will also be present for the other party's deposition, and that brings its own set of challenges and responsibilities. You absolutely cannot mentally check out while your attorney deposes your ex. There are certain things your attorney will depend on you to do as part of this process.

First, if you have not had your deposition taken yet, you need to pay very close attention to the process so it will not be as foreign and intimidating to you when it is your turn. Going first is hard because you won't know what to expect. If you have the chance to sit in on the other party's deposition first, a lot of the mystery and fear of the unknown will be washed away—assuming, of course, you pay attention.

Second, you should always be aware of your body language. Strive to maintain a poker face, no matter what you hear coming out of your ex's mouth. It may be difficult at times but try as hard as you can to suppress any shock, anger, disbelief, and so on. Your face and your body language provide a lot of information to the opposing party's attorney, even when you are not the one being questioned. Do not give them anything they can use against you, especially insight into how they might be able to get under your skin in later depositions or at trial.

Third, take notes. A lot of notes. *Very detailed* notes. Even though you are not the one being questioned, you are still an active participant in the deposition. You are there to help. You are going to hear some things in the other party's answer that may not mean anything to your attorney but mean a whole lot to you. You need to be able to note that and relate it to your lawyer later. And by the way, what is said about notes while you are being deposed doesn't apply to notes you take when someone else is being deposed. They belong to you and your attorney.

If you need to pass information to your attorney about answers they are getting from the other party, wait for a break unless your lawyer has told you otherwise. It is a good idea to ask them before the deposition how they want you to relay important information. Unless they've told you to, do not interrupt their process or flow by whispering in their ear or passing them a note. Generally, an attorney will not want you to interrupt them or derail their train of thought midway through the questioning, but they definitely need to know if you caught something that didn't sound right or if there is an issue or question they need to follow up on.

The Golden Rule for Depositions

Finally, as you head into your deposition, we want you to keep "the Golden Rule for Depositions" in mind: You cannot *win* a case in a deposition—but you can definitely *lose* one. You must be on guard about how you are feeling throughout the deposition and take breaks when you need it.

When the opposing attorney is questioning you in a deposition, they are getting a crystal-clear picture about how forceful you will be in fighting the allegations and how good (or bad) you will be on the witness stand at trial. If you make a poor showing in a deposition, it is a strong indication that you will make a poor showing at trial. On the other hand, if you do a great job fielding the questions, the opposing attorney may want to keep this case out of the courtroom and try to convince their client to settle.

Keep the Goal in Mind

Often people enter litigation scared to death of the actual *trial* part of the experience, but as we've seen, it's really the discovery phase that is more likely to take the wind out of our sails. By this point in the process, it's normal to feel mentally, emotionally, and physically exhausted. This is a perfect time to remind you what you're fighting for: your children and your ability to parent them effectively and in cooperation with their other parent. No matter how bad things may get, don't lose sight of the fact that you are fighting *for* your kids, not *against* your ex. That one attitude shift can keep you focused on the ultimate goal, which is not to win; it's to find the solution you can live with and is best for your child. Keep that goal in mind as we head into the next chapter, which will bring the rollercoaster back into the station through the trial, verdict, and possible appeal.

Chapter 7

THE TRIAL, VERDICT, AND APPEAL

We are in the thick of things now. Lawyers have been retained, papers have been served, and discovery is finished or underway. Are we having fun yet?

No?

Well, we have good news and bad news. The bad news is that it looks like you and your ex are heading to court. The good news, though, is that you still have an escape hatch. You've been through the wringer already, but you and your family can still get out of this with a solution that hits our goal of an outcome that is in the best interest of your child and is something you can live with. In this chapter, we'll remind you briefly how to end this mess *today,* and then we'll finish our discussion of the Execution phase for those who intend to see this all the way through to a trial (and maybe beyond).

Stages of a Typical Modification Case

1. Petitioner (the one initiating the lawsuit) hires a lawyer.

2. Petitioner draws up lawsuit papers.

3. Petitioner files the lawsuit with the court.

4. Petitioner has the papers served.

5. Respondent answers the suit.

6. Pre-trial motions and hearings.

7. Discovery process.

You are here

8. Negotiation.

9. Trial preparation.

10. Trial proceedings.

11. Rendition (the judge or jury renders a verdict).

12. Final order drawn up by the attorneys and signed by the judge.

13. Appeal process.

Execution Phase Step 8: Negotiation

The discovery step, which we discussed at length in the previous chapter, is a painful eye-opener for many people. Most people expect it to be mentally, physically, and emotionally taxing. But what shocks many families is how much time the discovery process takes and how ridiculously expensive it can be. Even those who begin the litigation with guns blazing usually have a "come-to-Jesus moment" during the discovery process. They realize, maybe for the first time, how great a toll this litigation is taking and will continue to take on everyone involved—including the children. If negotiating a settlement initially felt like a cop-out, this is usually the point when people start warming up to the idea of ending their case as quickly as possible. To use the highway analogy again, this is when they start looking for the next exit ramp that will get them off this trying journey. Suddenly, maybe for the first time, mediation becomes a viable option.

We discussed mediation in Chapter 1 primarily from the perspective of *avoiding* litigation altogether. Now is a great time to remember, though, that mediation is *always* an option at *any time* in the process. If you've made it this far and just want this nightmare to end, and if you and your co-parent haven't at least tried to negotiate an agreement, now could be the perfect time. Sometimes, warring factions need to take a few hits before they're willing to discuss a peace treaty. In the scope of your litigation journey, the period during or just after the discovery process—especially the depositions—could be *exactly* what both parties in your lawsuit need to bring them to the negotiating table.

If you are this far into things, and if you are willing to settle (or think your ex may finally be ready to settle), bring this option back up with your attorney. In many cases, the lawyers themselves can hash out a settlement agreement without even having to engage a mediator. You could be done with all this by the end of the week! But if you or your ex still can't or won't settle, and if you're heading into a trial, you and your legal team must prepare. That brings us to the next step in the process.

Execution Phase Step 9: Trial Prep

Now it's time to get ready to go to court. The trial prep phase is an extremely busy time for your attorney, but not nearly that busy for you. You, as the client, probably won't need to do much as long as your attorney has everything they need from you.

Your primary job during this pre-trial window, besides doing *whatever* your attorney tells you to do, is to study the discovery materials, starting with the transcript of your own deposition. You'll need to learn that transcript inside-out and front-to-back. This is where most of the questions you'll be asked on the witness stand will come from. Your attorney is building their case around your sworn deposition testimony and the discovery materials that have been collected. You need to be familiar enough with everything so you can give complete answers to the questions asked in the courtroom and ensure your sworn deposition and your courtroom testimony are in perfect harmony. You do not need to memorize everything or script your courtroom responses—that will make you come across like a robot in court—but you do need to be comfortable with and have a command of the facts you've presented.

This comfort level with your deposition responses will serve you well not only when your attorney is questioning you in court, but perhaps more importantly, when the opposing lawyer is cross-examining you. They, too, will develop a set of questions for you based on your deposition, and they would love nothing more than to catch you in a discrepancy between your deposition testimony and your testimony on the stand. If they catch you stating something in court that doesn't match what you said in your deposition, you can be accused of lying, changing your testimony, or any number of other terrible things. Your entire case could be jeopardized by a single inconsistency, so study, study, study!

You also want to study the other party's deposition, documents, and interrogatories. This is one of the biggest pain points of the entire litigation process for two reasons: It will be emotionally difficult reading everything your ex has said about your relationship, about you personally, and about your fitness as a parent. It will also be difficult to go through the sheer volume of material. Not only must you carefully review your ex's answers to all the interrogatory questions your attorney sent to them, but you will also need to review the pertinent documents they provided. It can be a mountain of material to work through, and you can't afford to "zone out" during any of it. Every sentence on every page demands your utmost attention. That level of attention to detail in addition to the anxiety of the case can and will wear you down over time.

The reason your attorney will want you to go over the opposing party's discovery material is because you will see things that your lawyer and their team might miss. Since you are so closely connected with the people and events of your case, you are the best one to call out to your attorney important statements, claims, and details from the discovery evidence and make sure they know to follow up on them.

As you go through the transcripts from the various depositions, don't be entirely shocked if you catch a mistake. Generally, there are two types of mistakes you might catch: First, the court reporter might have simply misheard or mistakenly transcribed your response. In this case, you are taking issue with the accuracy of the transcribed testimony. Second, and a bit more worrisome, you may read your testimony back and realize that you were mistaken in how you answered a question. Hopefully, this was just an honest mistake caused by misremembering something when asked in the high-pressure deposition setting. Either way, you have a bit of a problem on your hands: part of your sworn testimony, which both sides are building their cases around, is wrong! What do you do?

Do not panic. This happens more often than you'd think. Yes, the opposing counsel may try to use that mistake to their client's advantage, but these things usually aren't that big of a deal as long as you catch them early and make an honest effort to correct the record.

Technically, the deposition is the deposition. It can't really be changed. It can, however, be amended. You can amend the transcript by having your lawyer send something to the opposing party that says something to the effect of, "In my client's deposition testimony of April 19, on page 50, line 4 of the transcript, we want to amend our response." Then, provide the correct information. Again, you can't really change that deposition testimony per se, but you can certainly mitigate any damage if you realize later that your testimony was incorrect.

How the Lawyers Prepare for Trial

While you're studying the depositions and other discovery materials, your attorney will be hard at work building their case. Over time, individual attorneys develop their own system for trial prep, but it usually follows a similar flow and covers the same basic elements:

Develop a Theme for the Case

Early in their preparation for trial, your attorney will likely develop a *theme* for the case. This is the big picture, the overarching story the lawyer wants to present to the judge or jury at trial. Judges and jury members are human beings, and human beings connect with *stories* more than *facts*. Yes, the facts are important, but a good lawyer will find a way to present those facts in a narrative way that brings life to the story of the case they're trying to "sell" the court.

Amend Pleading and Discovery Responses (if Necessary)

By this point, all the relevant facts of the case should have been brought out of the shadows and into the light of day. With this new, complete picture of events, your attorney may realize their original pleading or some positions you took in discovery at the start of the case are no longer sufficient. They may wonder, *Does what we asked for at the start of the case still make sense in light of everything we now know? Should we pull some things back? Should we ask for more than we originally thought?* The pleading and positions you took in discovery will still be the driving force of the case, so your attorney will need to make sure they are still accurate. If something needs to change, your attorney can take steps to amend the pleading and amend or supplement your discovery responses.

As we've said, if you or your attorney catches an error in the discovery materials and/or deposition transcripts, now is the time to mitigate.

Fill Any Holes in the Discovery Materials

If everyone has done their job correctly during discovery, there should be no big surprises in the courtroom. It isn't like what you see in TV shows and movies. Generally speaking, both attorneys already know the answers to every significant question they intend to ask. They've seen every relevant document that might be offered into evidence. They know everyone who is even potentially related to the case and have had the opportunity to interview or depose them (with the major exception of *rebuttal witnesses,* who can be called to rebut a party's testimony on the stand, and potential *character witnesses,* whose testimony is not critical or maybe whose importance doesn't rise to the level of justifying the cost of deposing them). The old lawyer's maxim really is true: Never ask a question, especially of a hostile (unfriendly to your case) witness, unless you already know what the answer is.

Of course, all this depends on whether the attorney's discovery materials are complete. As your legal team is constructing their case, they should be asking themselves, "Do all these discovery materials support the theme/story we are developing? Were all the interrogatories we submitted sufficiently answered? Were all the disclosure requests and requests for production of documents sufficiently responded to? Have *we* supplied everything the other party properly requested?"

Both sides are using this time to prepare their cases. If there are any holes left over from discovery, now is the time to fill them!

Begin Organizing the Case

A big part of the legal team's preparatory work is to get the giant pile of discovery material organized. Again, different attorneys develop different preferences and styles, but typically a lawyer will have the deposition transcripts, interrogatory responses, and requested documents thoroughly indexed, filed, and cross-referenced to the questions they plan on asking. The goal is to create a system whereby they can instantly put their hands on any piece of evidence or any line of deposition testimony at a moment's notice at any point during the trial.

Prepare a Question Outline for Each Witness

Your attorney will prepare a list of questions for you and each friendly witness they intend to call to make their case and a list of cross-examination questions for the opposing party and each witness they think the opposing lawyer intends to call or might call. Ideally, these questions are indexed to the relevant pieces of evidence and deposition testimony so the attorney can bring each piece of the case into the trial at the appropriate time. This also enables your lawyer to pounce on any discrepancy in the other party's testimony on the stand.

We mentioned the potential rebuttal witness above. Here is where some surprises could pop up. The attorneys should be able to assume that you and your witnesses will tell the truth. If that doesn't happen, you have no room to complain about being surprised when a rebuttal witness takes the stand to refute the truthfulness of evidence you and your lawyer presented to the court.

Dennis

If I have the opposing party on the stand and they give me the wrong answer to a question I ask, meaning it's different than what they said in their deposition, then I'm going to stop everything and call them out on the spot. Whenever I ask a question in court, I'm looking at the page and line in their deposition where they've already answered that question. If they say something different in court, I'll approach them, hand them my binder, point out the relevant lines of their deposition transcript, and ask them to read it aloud to the court. I'll make it very clear they are giving a different answer now than they did then. Judges and juries don't like it when someone lies, either in their deposition or in court. It's a bad look, and it always hurts that side's credibility. Any lawyer worth their salt is going to take advantage of those opportunities to blow a hole in the opposing side's case.

———————

Prepare Client Testimony

As you get closer to trial, your lawyer should start walking you through your testimony and instructing you on how to answer specific questions in court. Some lawyers are much more methodical than others about it, but this is an important process for everyone to go through. These sessions give you the chance to hear what your lawyer is going to ask you on the witness stand and gives you some practice at answering those questions and being cross-examined. Of course, all this costs you time and money, but it is time and money well spent when heading into a trial, especially if this is the first time you've ever been to court.

Practice is important, but as we've said, be careful not to memorize all your answers. This will cause you to come across as too rehearsed, which can in turn make people wonder if you're being genuine or simply *playing the part* on the stand. Besides, things change quickly in a courtroom. If you have over prepared for one scenario, but that scenario suddenly flies out the window, you'll be stuck stammering for answers in front of the court. That looks much worse than being too prepared, because then you will look like you're trying to *make up* an answer.

The key is to be prepared and extremely familiar with your testimony but not scripting your answers to recite verbatim. That's far too risky and almost never works out the way you think it will.

Subpoena Witnesses

Finally, your lawyer will determine if there are witnesses who need to be subpoenaed. Obviously, you need to subpoena witnesses who would not come to court voluntarily. However, there may be some witnesses who don't want to be seen as voluntarily trying to help one side, so they would actually prefer to be subpoenaed to remove the illusion of choice. This is especially helpful for individuals who have good relationships with both parties in a case and do not want to look like they are favoring one side over the other.

Your attorney will be doing all these things and more to prepare for trial, so do whatever they ask you to do, respond to their inquiries as quickly and thoroughly as you can, and try not to bombard them with unnecessary phone calls, text messages, and emails while they are getting everything together. Stay on top of things, but also try to stay out of their way. They're doing a lot of work for you, and every minute they spend working on, talking about, or thinking about your case is costing you money!

UNDERSTANDING THE DOCKET AND COURT DATES

Before we leave the trial prep phase of your litigation journey, let's take a moment to understand how *court dockets* work. Otherwise, there's a good chance you'll go crazy wondering why your case hasn't been called yet.

In most instances, your case will be on a trial docket. A *docket* is simply a list of cases that need to be handled during a specific window of time. It could be a one-week docket, a two-week docket, or even a one-month docket. So, if it's a two-week docket and yours is one of five cases on that docket, that means the court will start and finish all five cases within two weeks.

This can be a bitter pill for someone to swallow. A family court lawsuit is one of the worst moments in someone's life. By the time they get to their court date, they've been unable to think about anything else for months. It seems like the biggest, scariest thing in the world. It can be difficult in that moment to fully accept the fact that your case, as enormous and all-encompassing as it is *for you*, is just one of many cases the court may be dealing with that week. The worst day of your life could be "just another day" to the people around you. It doesn't seem right or fair, but that's what litigation is like.

The most helpful warning we can give you here is to be extremely flexible with any dates provided. In some courts, your attorney might be able to get a special setting for your case to start on a specific date, but don't count on it. You may expect to start on a Monday, but your case may not be called until Wednesday. Your case may be delayed or paused while the court addresses any emergency hearings for your case or another case on the same docket. You or the opposing party in your case may need to file a motion for continuance, which means you simply aren't ready for the trial to start, or it could be that your attorney or opposing counsel has a scheduling conflict with another of their trials. (In many courts, the first motion for continuance is *automatically* granted.) Some courts only hear cases Monday through Thursday and focus on motions to enforce on Fridays. It all depends on the rules and the particular preferences of your court and jurisdiction.

The bottom line when it comes to dockets and court dates is this: Throughout the leadup to the trial and even *during* the trial, you may be given a lot of different dates for a lot of different things. Any one of them can be pushed to a different time, so you need to stay flexible and not pin all your hopes on any one date. It's like having dinner at a busy, understaffed restaurant—you know you'll get served eventually, but you're going to have to wait a while.

Execution Phase Step 10: Trial

Walking into a courtroom for the first time as the party to a contested lawsuit is one of the most intimidating experiences most people can ever have. Whether it's a business matter, civil suit, or family court issue, no one *wants* to have all their dirty laundry aired in front of a judge or jury, cross their fingers, and hope these strangers don't wreck their lives. Day One of a trial can make you feel like a five-year-old child walking into your first day of school: nothing is really what you imagined it would be, you don't know where to go, and all the "grown-ups" around you don't seem to understand or appreciate how frightening this is for you. Well, we do. So, let's dispel the mystery and intimidation by breaking down exactly what the trial process looks like.

We'll start with the basics. When you walk into the courtroom, you'll almost certainly see a raised desk in the front center of the room facing out. That's the *bench*, where the judge sits and presides over the proceedings. To one side of the bench is the *witness stand*, where witnesses sit to give testimony during the trial. Your attorney will lead you to what's usually called the *counselor's table*. This is where you'll sit for the duration of the trial. Typically, there are two counselor's tables on each side of the room facing the bench—one for the petitioner and one for the respondent. You'll sit at this table with your attorney and maybe an associate attorney for the duration of the case. Often, the parties in the case will sit on the outside seats of their respective counselor's tables, placing them as far away from each other as possible.

You'll notice a handful of other people posted in various places throughout the courtroom. The court reporter will be set up at a small desk, often between the bench and the parties. You'll see this person typing away throughout the trial, and they may not say a word (unless the judge or a lawyer in the case asks them to read back prior testimony from the record or the judge asks them if they need a break). A bailiff usually stands off to the side of the judge to keep an eye on everyone. Behind the counselor's tables and facing the front of the courtroom are usually seats or pews for spectators. This area is called the *gallery*. If you have people coming to support you during the trial, this is where they'll sit.

Trial Process

A typical trial will feel like a series of starts and stops. Lawyers will raise objections; the judge will call recesses; everything will grind to a halt while you wait on the attorneys and judge to argue about different motions; or the judge may break early for the day to attend to a more pressing matter in another case. There may be hours or entire days when you feel like nothing meaningful is happening at all. As frustrating as that can be, it's all part of the process—and that process has a fairly standard flow. You can trace the progression of your trial once you know the order of events:

Opening Statements

Each side is usually allowed to make an opening statement, which is their first word regarding the case. Here, they tell the judge and jury (if applicable) what to expect from them during the trial. They are not making their case here; rather, they're simply kicking things off, introducing the elements of their case and their client, and hoping to endear themselves to the factfinder (the judge or jury). Your attorney may choose to waive their opening statement, or, in some cases, if there is no jury, the judge may not want to hear opening statements. If statements are allowed, the petitioner's side goes first.

Petitioner Presents Their Case

The petitioner, sometimes called the *moving party*, makes their case first, presenting the themes they have prepared. This means the petitioner's attorney goes through their list of witnesses and lays out their case for why the modification needs to happen. The respondent's attorney has the chance to cross-examine each of these witnesses, but the respondent is not necessarily making their case yet; they are only responding to testimony given by the petitioner's witnesses. The petitioner ends their turn by resting their case. Occasionally, due to scheduling issues, the judge will allow a witness to testify out of order. For example, the respondent could be allowed to call a witness before the petitioner has concluded their case-in-chief (their side of the case before any rebuttal).

Respondent Asks for a Directed Verdict.

This step may or may not happen, depending on the responding attorney's preferences. Once the petitioner has closed their case, it is common for the respondent's attorney to automatically ask for a directed verdict. This means they want the judge to agree that the petitioner failed to prove their case as a matter of law and therefore end the trial right there. This is typically denied.

Respondent Makes Their Case

Assuming the request for a directed verdict is denied, the respondent's side then makes their case by arguing the themes they have prepared, calling their witnesses, and presenting their evidence. The petitioner's attorney also has the opportunity to cross-examine witnesses.

Petitioner Presents Rebuttal

Because the petitioner has the burden of proof, they are given the opportunity to rebut the respondent's case with rebuttal testimony.

Each Party Closes Their Case

The trial wraps up with closing arguments, with the petitioner again going first. The court may or may not want to hear final arguments, and some courts prefer *written* closing arguments which means the attorneys submit a written argument instead of presenting it verbally in court. Closing arguments are not allowed to reference anything that is outside the evidence that was presented; they simply argue the facts as they were presented to the court and how the law applies to the facts without bringing in any new information.

That's pretty much it. It seems straightforward when you look at the process neatly arranged in a list of steps like this, but it feels a lot messier and maybe even chaotic when you're actually sitting in the courtroom watching everything happen while your parental rights and access to your children are on the line.

One more thing we should mention here is that there are typically time limits during a trial. The court *always* wants to end one case as quickly and efficiently as possible to move onto the next one on the docket. While this might be a once-in-a-lifetime experience for you, the judge may need to get through three other cases by the end of the week. Thus, they want to keep things moving. This means each lawyer is always having to watch the clock and make judgment calls about when to press in on something and when to let something go. They may choose to pull some things out of your case that you'd love to have presented in order to spend time on the things they think are most compelling. This is a major reason why you want an experienced attorney representing you. Lawyers with little experience in trying a family law case may spend their precious time on the wrong issues in the case. Everything matters, but only an experienced professional will know what matters *most*.

Decorum in the Courthouse

We talked at length about decorum during depositions in the previous chapter. Every one of those suggestions applies even more to the actual trial. You are on stage from the moment you pull into the courthouse parking lot in the morning to the moment you drive away at the end of the day. You must be cognizant of everything you say and do, from verbal statements to body language. It is not just about what happens inside the actual courtroom, either; you never know who is going to see you in the hallway, run into you in the elevator, or overhear a conversation you have in the bathroom. Every word you say and every person you encounter in and around that building represents an opportunity to help or hurt your case.

When you are in the courtroom itself, you must be polite, use proper etiquette, speak respectfully and articulately, and control any body language that could give a negative impression. No matter what you're feeling internally, you've got to keep a poker face. This means:

- No eye rolling.
- No scowling, side-eye, or dirty looks.
- No moans and groans when the other party is giving testimony.
- No speaking while someone is giving testimony. (There should be no speaking at all when you are at the counselor's table, except for whispering to your attorney at the appropriate times.)
- No speaking/interrupting when someone else is talking, especially the judge or lawyers.
- No frantically scribbling down notes at the counsel's table so angrily and aggressively that you are leaving permanent indentations in the table and everyone in the courtroom can hear your pen strokes!

Of course, we are not suggesting you act like a dead-eyed robot. This trial will certainly bring up some emotions and will cover some very emotional topics. Do not be afraid to show *some* emotional reaction, but do not be overly dramatic. Do whatever it takes to suppress any outward expressions of anger, disgust, and so on.

You also need to appear engaged throughout the trial. Listen intently to each witness and take good notes. If you hear something that is meaningful to you, especially if it is something your attorney may not have caught, make a note and get that information to your lawyer at the appropriate time. Discuss with them beforehand how they want you to communicate this information on the fly. However, be extremely careful with any notes you make. Keep everything on a legal pad, and keep that legal pad with you at all times. Some attorneys will literally go through the trash in the courthouse to retrieve scraps of paper if they see you throw something away.

Execution Phase Step 11: Rendition

Once the trial has closed, the next step is to receive the *rendition*, or the judge's verdict. The best-case scenario is that the judge will render the verdict immediately at the conclusion of the trial while everyone is still there in person. While that does happen occasionally, it's more likely that you will leave the courthouse with no verdict and then wait for the rendition to arrive, which could take days or even weeks. The delay could be because the judge is either tied up with other cases or has a question about the case but hasn't had time to research it. The judge may also want an opportunity to go back and review some evidence. The wait could be caused by *anything,* and you will have no idea what is taking so long. It can be maddening.

The big problem (aside from your sanity) is that the further the judge gets from actually hearing the evidence that was presented, the more they forget. Also, the judge is still hearing other cases while you are waiting on a ruling, which means they're hearing a ton of detailed evidence about other families. As you wait for a final decision, you risk having other cases obfuscate what the judge remembers about you and your family. Oftentimes, if the parties are left waiting too long, the lawyers in the case may start introducing random post-trial motions just to get the case back on the judge's radar and (hopefully) encourage them to make a ruling.

If the rendition isn't given immediately in court, it will usually be delivered to the attorneys electronically, essentially as an email notice that the judge has rendered a verdict. That verdict is usually in line with the requests made in the pleadings or countersuit in the case. It would be very unusual (but not impossible) for the judgment to go far afield from what the parties were seeking.

Execution Phase Step 12: Final Orders

It would be understandable to assume that once the judge renders a final ruling, everything is finished. Not so! Even though the judge has decided the case, that rendition still needs to be written into new court orders to replace the prior orders. This is typically referred to as *drawing up final orders*, which is usually done by the lawyers in the case, rather than the judge. The judge might instruct the attorney for the petitioner or the perceived "winning party" to prepare the final order for entry, in which case the attorney for the other party would have an opportunity to object to the order as written and point out changes they think should be made to accurately reflect the rendition of the court. In the absence of directives from the court as to who should draw up the final orders, each attorney can submit their proposed set of final orders.

If the attorneys have a disagreement about the specific language in the proposed judgment, they will have one (hopefully) final appearance before the court. The parties in the case don't usually need to be present for this, however. This is not an occasion for any new testimony or evidence; it is simply a time for the attorneys to argue interpretation issues regarding the judgment and to let the judge ultimately decide between them. Usually the judge will then instruct one of the lawyers to incorporate that decision into the final orders before sending the judge and opposing counsel a draft to review and approve. Once the judge signs off on the new orders, they go into effect and become enforceable by the court, superseding the prior orders. Any temporary orders not incorporated into the final orders go away as though, going forward, they were never in effect.

As the lawyers hash out the details for the final order draft, we strongly encourage you to build in a dispute resolution process for future disagreements. By the time you've reached the end of your trial, the last thing you *ever* want to do is to go through all this again with your ex. You can take steps toward avoiding that by planning ahead to include mediation requirements into your new orders. That way, you won't be surprised in a few years by another process server showing up at your front door with a new lawsuit. Instead, you and your ex will be bound to follow the mediation plan outlined in your new orders.

Execution Phase Step 13: Appeal

The last step in the Execution phase is one that may or may not happen: the appeal. Appeals are difficult and expensive, and it is even more difficult to have a case successfully reversed on appeal in a family case. For this reason, appeals made on trial to the court custody modifications appeals are not that common. (Trial by jury is more likely to be appealed, as evidentiary errors could lead to a reversal.)

In Texas (where we are), any evidence that was improperly admitted in a trial to the court is irrebuttably presumed not to have been considered by the judge in making their decision. That means even if evidence was admitted that might have swayed the judge in one direction or the other, the irrebuttable presumption is that this material was not considered by the in such a way as to affect the outcome. To have an effective appeal, you need to be able to prove that the judge not only erred, but that the error rose to the level of being an abuse of discretion.

You ultimately have the test of what is in the best interest of the child. This is of utmost importance to the court, but it is also a gray area, and you could say is even subjective in essence. It calls for the factfinder (the judge in a non-jury trial) to weigh the credibility and veracity of the witnesses—something that's hard to do from the appellate court's review of only the written record of the case. Each party is likely to have some disagreement over what is in the best interest of the child, and the judge may see things differently than either party. Even if you believe you have an appealable issue, the appellate court may (and probably will) disagree.

There is one key difference in an appeal compared to the initial custody case: in an appeal, you are no longer arguing *facts*; you are arguing *law* and how the law is applied to the specific set of facts that was presented at trial. For this reason, the appeal is in the hands of the attorneys. The parties themselves don't have much to do during an appeal because there's no opportunity for new evidence or testimony once the case goes to an appellate court. It's all about lawyers arguing the law.

If you do go down the road of appeals, you are probably going to need to bring in a different attorney and possibly a different law firm. An appellate proceeding is quite different from a trial to the court and therefore needs an attorney experienced in handling appeals. There are lawyers whose primary practice area is appellate law, and who take cases after they have been tried in the trial court. When money is not an object, they are sometimes hired to work with the trial lawyer from the inception of the case.

The appeals process is a minefield, and you need to know what you're doing. A lawyer who is not used to handling appeals won't be that valuable to you because they will not be as familiar with the unique obstacles, time limits, and technicalities regarding preparing and presenting a case at the appellate level. Of course, this type of specialty experience and training comes at a high cost. For this and several other reasons, including the cost of having the entire proceeding transcribed from the court reporter's stenographic notes, appeals are extremely expensive even though they are usually unsuccessful.

We are not saying you should never consider filing an appeal; we just want to stress that this is a very different process with a low success rate and steep price tag that requires a lawyer with a high degree of specialty training to handle things properly. With these factors in mind, if you still think an appeal is a good option, discuss it first with your trial attorney. If he or she agrees with you, ask them for recommendations on a good lawyer that specializes in appeals.

Also keep in mind that you might unwillingly find yourself in appeals territory if the opposing party in your case pursues an appeal. If that happens, you have little choice but to find an attorney seasoned in handling appeals and prepare a defense. If there is a wide financial gap between the losing party and the winning party (i.e., the losing party has more money), the losing party may pursue an appeal simply to financially harm the other party. It's sad but true—especially in situations in which one parent seems to care more about getting revenge on their ex than what is best for their child.

Living The Litigation

Scott

Over the past few chapters, Dennis and I have tried to prepare you for the nuts and bolts of your litigation by unpacking each step of the journey. It may have come across as cold and clinical at times because we've been focused on the *process*, not the *people*. That's easy for us because we are not in the thick of things like you are. But don't let the practical, tactical, how-to nature of this section of the book fool you. We are not coming at this as two guys who are clueless about how stressful and painful the custody litigation experience is. Dennis has walked hundreds of families through this nightmare on the legal side, and I've helped hundreds of families through it on the counseling side. Additionally, as I've mentioned, my family spent more than a year living the "litigation lifestyle" when my stepson's father took us to court. I have been where you are. I have had those same sleepless nights, lying in bed with my stomach in knots listening to my wife weep and whimper quietly beside me. I have cried with my wife in fear of losing our son's love, if not his custody. I have been so angry that I've wanted to punch holes in walls, and so mad that I could barely speak. I remember how hard it was to keep a level head and trust the legal process when all I wanted to do was scream. Yes, I know the difference between *talking* about the Execution phase and *living* the Execution phase.

If there is any encouragement as you walk this road, it is this: your litigation will not last forever. There is a light at the end of the tunnel. There will be a day when your lawsuit is *not* the first thing you think about when you wake up, the last thing you think about before falling asleep, and the only thing you dream about in between. Even if you do not get the result you want, a day is coming when life will be "normal" again ... whatever that means for you.

Readjusting to life beyond litigation—and healing from the wounds caused by it—are the topics of the next section of the book, entitled Recovery. First, we'll discuss how to regain some sense of normalcy in your own home, experience personal healing, and reconnect with your spouse and children. Then, we'll explore what may seem unthinkable: getting back to a healthy, working relationship with your co-parent, despite what they may have just put your family through.

Take a breath. The trial is over. Now, it's time to get back to your life.

Section 3

RECOVERY

Chapter 8

RESETTING YOUR LIFE

Welcome to the Recovery phase. We're glad you are (finally) here.

The Recovery phase begins once you've put everything in the litigation process to bed and can start redirecting your time, attention, and energy toward resetting your life and moving forward. In other words, this is when you'll start spending more time with your family than with your lawyer!

Of course, you must make sure everything is signed, finalized, and filed with the court before you wish your attorney well and send them on their way. Do not assume all of this will be taken care of for you. Talk to your lawyer and make sure you understand exactly what is happening and *who* was responsible for *what*. You don't want any loose ends left that may trip you up later on.

Also, you need to make sure your lawyer has been fully paid or is on a payment plan. You want to end your litigation well with your attorney and leave the door open just enough that you can still send them questions here and there as you move forward with your new custody orders. You should also get a copy of your new final orders and make sure you understand every line. Review any final questions with your attorney before saying goodbye.

With all that taken care of, it's time to take a breath.

Take A Breath

Scott

That first morning after our lawsuit was finally over was weird. It was a victory for us because we were so ready to be done with everything and stop worrying about it. My wife commented, "I don't have to live and parent under a microscope anymore. No one is going to attack my motherhood today!" That was huge for us. For the first time in a long while, we realized we were released from parenting from a position of fear.

There can be and should be a wonderful sense of relief when the litigation is over, even if you did not get the outcome you were hoping for. By this point, you have spent months living in daily stress, anxiety, anguish, and warfare. Once you reach the end of the Execution phase and enter Recovery, you should take a little time to appreciate the fact that the war is over, the dust is settling, and there are no more bullets whizzing by your head. There is a strange peace that comes over you when you know that part of the battle is over. Don't be afraid to enjoy that. Embrace it. You can finally take a deep breath.

It is important to enter into a season of rest as you come out of litigation. This is desperately needed for you as an individual, you and your spouse as a couple, and your family as a whole. You've been in freeze, fight, and flight mode for a long time. You've maintained a massive buildup of adrenaline, and suddenly it is over. It's like tensing a muscle nonstop for a solid year and then finally letting it relax. It slowly dawns on you, "Oh, wait. I'm not facing a deposition today. I don't have to do any research. I can literally do *whatever I want* today." Vanessa and I were suddenly freed up to put our focus back on the things we *wanted* to focus on, like our marriage and our three younger boys who had not received nearly the amount of attention they needed and deserved for the past year. My wife recently told me, "I don't remember Grayson being two years old. I don't have any clear memories of him at that age because my entire brain was focused on the lawsuit. That's not fair. It wasn't fair to him, and it wasn't fair to me as a mom." She's right. It wasn't fair. The litigation robbed us of so many other precious things that we *should* have been able to focus on instead of having to deal with this constant court battle with her ex. And coming out of it, we genuinely had to deal with the anger and frustration of this ordeal having stolen a chunk of our lives. Wherever you are in the process, you probably feel the same way. It's just not fair. But it's the battle we're sometimes called to fight as parents in a blended family.

Reconnection

When you're in the middle of a custody lawsuit, no matter what else is going on in your life at the time, the litigation is the thing that occupies your thoughts and lives more than anything else. It's an enormous boulder sitting in the middle of your life. Everything else you do—your job, your marriage, your other kids, your spiritual life, your social life—gets squeezed out to the edges of your custody case. It is the first thing you think of when you wake up in the morning and the last thing you think of before going to sleep at night. Then, suddenly—*finally*—it's gone. You're left with the lingering questions, "Who are we as a family now that this is settled? How will we move on with our lives? And how can we hope to have a comfortable co-parenting relationship with the other party after all the fighting, hard feelings, and terrible things we've said *to* each other and *about* each other throughout this mess?"

These are good questions. We'll deal with the second question—how to reengage with your co-parenting team—in the next chapter. For now, let's focus on resetting the relationships under your own roof. This includes the three key "reconnections" you'll need to make now that the litigation is behind you: reconnect with *yourself,* reconnect with *your spouse*, and reconnect with *your children*. You can't hope to have a healthy, effective co-parenting relationship with your ex if you haven't first covered these three bases in your own home.

Reconnecting With Yourself

Litigation causes people to do, say, and think things that shock even themselves. Even the sweetest, calmest person in the world can become a raging maniac after two hours of depositions! Add that to the constant pressure, endless anxiety, interpersonal drama, and outright fear that permeates the litigation process, let that build over the course of many months, and you will probably be left with a version of yourself that is at least a *little* unrecognizable. When the people we work with get to the end of their litigation journey, they're usually a mess. Some have described it like waiting for a bomb to go off as the pressure builds but then, instead of exploding, the pressure just fizzles out like a leaky balloon. There's no grand finale, no fireworks, no BOOM. Everything in them is still dialed up to eleven, but it's all over and they're left not knowing what to do with all the leftover emotions of anger, guilt, fear, sorrow, and confusion that have permeated every moment of their lives for so long.

A big part of the problem is that most families "circle the wagons" as the lawsuit progresses. We've talked about the importance of keeping your circle of trust—the group of people who have detailed information about your case—intentionally small, but that level of privacy takes a toll on most people. Instead of venting to friends, we let all that pressure build up. Many people, fearing they may let something slip, stop spending time with loved ones outside the immediate family. We've heard from so many couples exiting litigation that their biggest mistake was cutting themselves off from their community of friends and family. They were so busy, so stressed, and so worried about accidentally saying something that could hurt their case that they kept their heads down and let even their closest relationships grow cold.

We've stressed throughout this book the importance of having *someone* to talk to about everything that's happening, but we've also cautioned you about saying *too much* to *too many* people. That can be a frustrating and near-impossible balancing act, and many people err on the side of privacy. That might be good for the case, but it's bad for mental and emotional health. If this is a ball you've dropped during the litigation, it's the first one you need to pick up afterward. Obviously, this means reengaging in your extended family and friendships, church family, and other areas where you've planted social roots. It might also mean identifying a mentor—someone who's already been through a tough family litigation and come out the other side. But the most important interpersonal relationship you can build at this time—outside your heavenly Father and family, of course—is a one-on-one healing relationship with a counselor. Your inner life was blown to bits throughout this lawsuit, and you're going to need some help putting those pieces back together.

Post-Litigation Personal Counseling Goals

There are many different issues you may (and probably do) need to unpack with a professional counselor as you go through *and* as you come out of your litigation experience. We couldn't possibly cover or even name every counseling need someone in your position might have, but we can address the ones we've seen most often in the families we've worked with.

Probably the most common issue is *unresolved anger*. So many things happen and so many things are said during a lawsuit, and most of those things have the power to hurt and offend you. There is the obvious sources of anger, of course—the other party and their attorney—but some of the most painful and anger-inducing personal incidents are the result of "friendly fire" you took from someone who was supposed to be on your team. Maybe your spouse didn't support you the way you needed them to at a key point in the case. Maybe you're the stepparent in this situation, and you didn't feel as though your voice counted or was even heard. Maybe your child made untrue allegations against you or your spouse in order to sway the case the way *they* wanted it to go. These kinds of "friendly fire" attacks can hurt much more than anything the other party in the case could have said or done because we didn't see them coming and are not sure how to process the powerful feelings they evoke. If this sounds familiar, you are certainly not alone. This is a common situation in family lawsuits. Don't bury your anger, blame yourself for it, or take it out on your loved ones. Instead, let it all out in the safe confines of a counseling session. Any good counselor will have some wonderful strategies for getting past these very real and very painful wounds.

Another area you should explore in counseling is the issue of *inner vows*. An inner vow is a promise we make to ourselves, usually born of pain and frustration. Examples in a family law case might be:

- "I'm never going to speak to them again."
- "As soon as this kid turns 18, those people are out of my life forever."
- "We only have to do this for two more years, and then we're done with them."
- "I will only ever do what is required by the court orders and not one step further."
- "I will never forgive this person."
- "I won't allow God to lead me to a place of forgiveness or into a healthy relationship with this person."

Each of these statements may make perfect sense to us when we say them, but they all come with one big problem: When we make an inner vow about what we will or will not ever do again, we are trying to wrestle God's sovereignty out of His hands. We are telling Him what we will and will not allow Him to do. We are effectively kicking Him out of key areas of our lives. We're saying, "I—not God—will control how I'm going to engage in this relationship from now on." This is an attitude God can certainly *understand*, but it is not one He will *bless*. If you truly want to move forward into the rich, new, full life He has in store for you post-litigation, you've got to trust Him to lead you where He wants you to go—and that includes how and when your life will intersect with your ex. Search your heart for any inner vows you have made through your court battle, honestly unpack them with your counselor, and do whatever it takes to submit them to God.

The issue of guilt is another key counseling topic for people coming out of litigation. Guilt seems to permeate every part of the case nearly as much as anger does. There's guilt for putting your spouse through all of this. Guilt for how your child has treated their stepparent. Guilt for the lack of attention you've been able to give your children, especially any children from your new marriage who were not directly involved in the lawsuit. Guilt for the tremendous impact the case had on your family's financial goals. Guilt for fighting when you should have settled. Guilt for settling when you should have fought harder. Guilt for your impatience, for your harsh words, for your lack of intimacy with your spouse, for how the case impacted your productivity at work. There is so much guilt to go around! Search your heart for any tinges of guilt, state them clearly, and discuss them with your therapist. If you don't, the guilt can eat away at your heart like poison until there's nothing left.

A close cousin of guilt is *grief.* As you come out of litigation, you will likely go through a grieving process as you face a number of issues: the time that was lost; the damage that was done to all the different relationships affected by the case; the loss of the last goodwill you had for your ex; the fact that someone you once loved could have said *this* or done *that*; hurtful words your child may have said out of their own anger, fear, or confusion; stress that was put on your family; and so much more. The very existence of this lawsuit is evidence that something precious was lost, whether it was trust, confidence, respect, or any other reason that led to one party challenging the other's parental rights. That alone is worth grieving. Be honest about your grief. Your heart can and will heal, but only if you face the deep sense of loss within.

Other things you may need to discuss with a counselor over the course of many weeks or months could include:

- Removing fear from your daily life and parenting.
- Finding your safe space physically and emotionally.
- Carefully exploring your heart for any trace of post-traumatic stress that might silently grow in secret—until it explodes back to the surface sometime later when you least expect it.
- Second-guessing your actions and the decisions you made throughout the litigation and any agreements you made to end it.
- Processing what you discovered about yourself through this ordeal—the good (*I'm a lot stronger than I realized*), the bad (*I'm capable of a lot more anger than I thought*), and the ugly (*I can't believe I said **that**. What does that say about my relationship with God?*).

We cannot stress this enough: You *need* to book some time with a counseling professional to untangle the complicated web of feelings you are sure to have as you conclude your litigation journey. You'll see that we will also recommend a marriage counselor and a counselor for your children below, but your healing journey starts with *you*. Each individual in the case was individually affected in unique ways, and you each need time and space to work through it. You are most certainly worth it.

RECONNECTING WITH YOUR SPOUSE

The most heartbreaking outcome of a custody litigation is to win the case but lose your marriage in the process. You might think that sounds overly dramatic, or depending on how well your current marriage has weathered your own litigation, you might not think we are being dramatic *enough*. We've seen this happen enough to know the danger is real. If you're not careful, your custody modification case can blow a hole right through your marriage.

Ideally, you've attacked this litigation as a team and have supported each other every step of the way, giving each other extra helpings of grace when the courtroom drama had frazzled each of you to the last, thin, twitching little nerve. And hopefully, you miraculously managed to maintain a regular date night throughout the litigation journey. Whether you did or didn't, you definitely need to date your spouse now in the aftermath. This kind of experience changes individuals and families. If you are not intentional about staying connected with your spouse during the legal process and immediately afterward, you may realize one day soon that your spouse has become a completely different person when you weren't looking. You got to know them the first time by dating. Guess what? You *keep* getting to know them the same way.

Scott

You've probably also realized that communication is crucial to maintaining a healthy marriage during the lawsuit. Well, it's just as important after the case is closed. Coming out of our year of litigation, it was nice to be able to have a conversation with my wife that did not involve her ex-husband. For more than a year, every conversation we had involved him in some way. We had so many other things going on in our lives, yet her ex was hovering right there in the room with us wherever we were and whatever we were doing. I intend no offense to the guy, but I was so glad when we were able to kick him out of our date nights, phone calls, text messages, and dinner table discussions.

You need to communicate when you are frustrated, when you feel hopeless, when you are angry, and so on. It is too easy to pack all of this away in a dark corner of your heart and not talk about it. It is also common to put many things on the back burner of your marriage until the litigation is over, so you may have a pile of issues and unanswered questions that have been waiting for you to have time and space to address them. That time is now, so bring in a marriage counselor and create a safe place to unpack everything you've stored up during the litigation journey. Counseling also gives you a set time to have these discussions so you can be sure not to overlook them. Plus, counseling provides you an impartial, experienced third party to help you sort through these issues.

Some key topics to explore with a marriage counselor include:

- Working on strengthening communication.
- Strategies for conflict management.
- Dealing with any feelings of guilt for dragging the stepparent through such a stressful and expensive ordeal.
- Maintaining or reestablishing intimacy and making it a priority.
- How and why to institute (or reinstitute) a regular, no-kids date night.
- The need to get away with your spouse to reconnect and refresh yourselves.
- Reviewing the tremendous impact this litigation had on your family financial goals.

If you have never been to a marriage counselor, I cannot stress how important this can be to the long-term health and enjoyment of your marriage.

RECONNECTING WITH YOUR CHILDREN

We have said that there are no real winners in litigation, but there are definite losers: the children. As parents signed up to be a blended family; the children didn't really have a choice. As we have said before, the child is the one who has to deal with both sides of the litigation through the entire case. They never get a break from it. They are stuck in the middle of a situation they did not want and cannot control. Too often, in the worst cases, they hear each parent speaking poorly about the other parent all the time. This can and does lead to damaged parent-child relationships, loss of trust, hurt feelings, and anger. Repairing the damage and rebuilding bridges is a key part of the Recovery phase.

Coming out of litigation, you may realize your relationship with your children (those who were part of the litigation) is a little different than it was before. This is especially true if your child made crazy accusations and false claims during the case. Unfortunately, this is quite common. It is especially prevalent in situations where one parent is manipulating the child to take a position against the other parent. Even if what they say isn't true, kids can still be positioned to make outrageous claims against even the best parents. This is why parent alienation and child manipulation are such critical issues in these cases. Judges know the damage these things leave on families and therefore will not tolerate any trace of it in your case.

Further complicating the issue, these false claims, as hurtful and damaging as they are, sometimes come from a simple desire to have a better relationship with a parent. For example, a child who doesn't see her father very often may want to live with him full-time. She might think "the grass is greener" at her father's house, or she may feel like her father has always overlooked her and sees this as an opportunity to have a closer relationship with him. The father might have even encouraged this belief, telling the child that she *can* and *should* come live with him. In this situation, the girl isn't *trying* to hurt her mother. She's just genuinely seeking a closer relationship with her father. It's not a bad goal per se, but she's coming at it from a child's perspective. She doesn't know—she *can't* know—all the different reasons why a custody change may be a bad idea. From her perspective, it's a case of Mom not letting her get closer to Dad. So it's understandable that she would lash out at Mom in that situation, saying terrible things and even lying to the court to get the outcome she thinks she wants. And then, when the case is over, Mom has to figure out how to get past all that hurt and betrayal and reconnect with her little girl. It's really, really tough. And very, very common.

This is difficult enough if the child is young, but the nastiness can reach maximal levels if the child is older, especially in their teens. Teenagers can be more methodical in their manipulations and more hurtful in their words. Let's face it: teenagers can be horrible to deal with under the best of circumstances. Put them in a rough custody case, and things can go south quickly. You can come through this with a lot of leftover anger and zero trust in the child, especially if you are the stepparent who has only parented them for a few years. As hard as it is, you as the adult must willfully decide to put this ordeal behind you and move forward, even if that means starting from scratch with the child and redeveloping a brand-new new relationship.

Scott

Aside from the emotional and behavioral impact of the lawsuit on both children and parents, there are also practical changes to the child's living situation that often create more stress as everyone tries to adjust to the "new normal." Before my family's lawsuit, for example, our son lived with us full-time and spent every other weekend, one weeknight, and extended weeks during the summer with his father. As part of our litigation settlement, that changed to a 50/50 custody split in which our son lived with us for a week and his father for a week, rotating back and forth year-round. While

I personally think this is the best custody arrangement whenever possible (assuming there are no child-endangerment issues), this was a major change for our family.

From a practical standpoint, we had to figure out what it meant to have him living with us half the time and with his father half the time. Was he supposed to have two of everything—wardrobe, computers, game systems, etc.—so he didn't need to move a truckload of stuff back and forth every week? What if his grades suffered because his father wasn't as concerned as we were about making him do his homework? What if he left something important at his father's house? What would we all do if one parent grounded him for a month—should we expect his father to keep him grounded at his house because of something he did at ours?

Big changes like this, especially on the heels of a prolonged custody lawsuit, add a new layer of complexity to an already stressful situation. Navigating this new parenting landscape will take some time and patience.

_____

Invest in Counseling for the Children

Obviously, we recommend counseling for the children involved in the litigation, and it's best not to wait until the lawsuit is resolved. Kids need help processing what they are thinking and feeling throughout the case, not just when it's over. Many kids are "stuffers." They stuff a lot of their emotions and feelings—especially the painful ones—deep down. They need help to carefully unpack all of that and develop some healthy coping mechanisms for future conflict. Other kids may be much more reactionary and explosive. They too need help managing all the wild emotions that are stirred up throughout and after a custody case.

Family counseling can be great, but it should not take the place of giving your child quality, consistent, private, one-on-one time with a good counselor who specializes in children and teens. They need someone they can vent to and be brutally honest with—without worrying about Mom and Dad finding out what all they're saying. Of course, this means you've got to be comfortable having your child discussing whatever they need to talk about *without* you hounding them later to tell you everything they said in counseling. Their counseling sessions should be private, and you as the parent need to respect that privacy. The counselor is legally and ethically bound to tell you if the child might be a danger to themselves or others. Beyond that, give them their privacy. They need to get some things off their chest.

Now, just because they *need* it doesn't mean they'll *want* it. In fact, practically *no* child will want to see a counselor. They may only go kicking and screaming, so prepare for their resistance. You must also be willing to try out a few different counselors until you find one that fits. This needs to be someone your child feels comfortable opening up to. Otherwise, they won't get much value out of the opportunity.

If your child needs some convincing, it might help to say, "This doesn't mean there's anything wrong with you. This is just somebody that can be your personal life coach, someone you can tell anything you want. You can tell them if you're upset with me or if you're upset with your mom/dad/stepparent or whatever it is. You have a neutral party to talk to and who is not going to try to convince you of anything or expect you to pick sides. Plus, I'm not going to know anything about what you talk about in there, so take advantage of that." Of course, be extra careful to keep any promises you make to them about their privacy with the counselor. If they find out you went back on your word and tried to get the counselor to divulge what they discussed, it will ruin their trust not only in counseling but in you as their parent.

Still No Venting to Your Children!

If you successfully kept yourself from burdening your child with too much information (or gossip) throughout the litigation, congratulations! You did great! Now keep doing it.

It's strange how often parents hold their tongue throughout the lawsuit, maybe out of fear of giving the other party extra ammo to use against them, but then spill their guts to their children as soon as the case is resolved. It can feel like you've been holding your breath for months. Then, when the litigation is over, it can be a bit too easy to *finally* exhale in front of the children. A lot of stuff can come out with that long-held breath, and much of it does not support the goal of what's best for the child.

If you managed to keep the children out of it throughout the whole litigation, do not fool yourself into thinking it is okay to tell them everything now that it's over. You didn't just hold your tongue this long because it was in the best interest of your *lawsuit*, but because it was in the best interest of your *child*. That is still true even now that the case is finished. You won't be helping them by telling them what you *really* think of their other parent or by discussing your opinion of all the dirty tricks the other party played throughout the lawsuit.

That said, it is natural to ask the question, "When is it okay to tell my child everything that happened during the litigation?" Our answer is: when they're an adult. Unless there are serious issues like abuse, it is important to encourage the child to have a healthy relationship with the other parent. You cannot do that if you are also filling their ears with every terrible thing the other parent has said or done.

Of course, the children will probably ask one or both parents for details about what happened during the case. If or when they ask you, give them your honest answer: "I'll tell you whatever you want to know when you're 18."

Once the child reaches age eighteen, they can choose what kind of relationship they want to have with each parent. And, as adults, they deserve to have all the information they need to make a good decision. But at least give them the *full* story when you tell them, which means telling them how *you* behaved as well. There's no point hiding any of those potentially embarrassing details. Your ex will probably tell them anyway!

Model Grace and Stability

Going through this kind of experience can make a lasting impact on your children. Even if they seem mad at you the entire time, the litigation and recovery process gives you an incredible opportunity to model to your kids what a healthy marriage and healthy parenting look like. The litigation has already given them a window into what it looks like when relationships go terribly wrong. If you've remarried, you can balance that by showing them a healthy marriage and a wonderful picture of a relationship going well. The child may not appreciate that in the moment, but it will almost certainly be something they look back on later in life.

This is also a powerful opportunity to demonstrate your love for them by offering a place of stability. They've spent months trying to keep their balance in the ever-shifting sands of litigation. Now, by working hard to keep your home a place of safety and stability, you can give them the firm foundation they desperately need to get back on their feet and move past the nightmare they've just been through.

Ideally, your child will also come away from the litigation with an understanding of what sacrificial love looks like. As we've discussed through the process, you as the parent must make decisions that you don't necessarily *like* or *want* to do, but that you know are in the best interest of your child. Remember what we've said about the goal of litigation: it is a resolution you can live with and that is in the best interest of the child. *The child* is the focus of that goal. They get what's best; you as the parent only get something you can live with.

Hopefully, they will come to appreciate those sacrifices as you all heal together.

Chapter 9

RESETTING
THE PARENTING TEAM

As you go through litigation, it is natural to put up a false face. We aren't talking about lying to anyone. We are talking more about how you *present* yourself. It's almost like you're walking through things wearing a bulletproof vest. You're trying to look like things aren't affecting you as much as they really are, like you are impervious to all the slings and arrows being hurled at you.

Because each party is so aware of how they are acting and what image they are portraying, it can be difficult for anyone to understand what the other side is *truly* feeling during and after the case concludes. You might think the other party was completely unaffected because they never let their feelings show in your interactions. But the person who seemed so calm, cool, and collected in the courtroom or at the mediation table could have been—and probably was—an emotional wreck at home when they could be real.

Isn't this what you did yourself? Didn't you try to mask the pain, anger, confusion, fear, anxiety, doubt, and outright panic each step of the way?

You must assume the other party did it too.

This aura of invulnerability is important during your case. Your attorney probably even coached you not to let your raw emotions pour out or to give the opposing counsel any sign that they got under your skin. *We've* even coached you to do that in earlier chapters of this book! The problem is, as important as this "stiff upper lip" is during the case, it can make it impossible to know how your co-parent is really feeling during and, more importantly, coming out of the litigation.

As we've said throughout this book, as nasty as the litigation may get, you're going to need to find some way to still parent alongside this person after the lawsuit is behind you. No matter what they've said about you or how you've acted toward them, your children still need you to set all that aside and come together as a parenting team.

For this reason, we recommend touching base with the other party very soon after the litigation is over for what we call a *temperature check*. This is simply an opportunity to have an honest conversation about how you are each feeling about things now that the case is closed. Ideally, this would be a face-to-face meeting, such as having all the parents and stepparents meet for coffee or lunch. That may be (and probably is) the last thing you want to do. It might seem like a miserable and impossible task, and the other party might refuse. That's okay too. Don't force this on anyone. But if you are all able and willing to come together for a discussion for the sake of your children, it can go a long way to resetting the relationship in a positive way.

This kind of temperature check meeting might surprise you. It is so easy to assume the worst about the other party as you work through a lawsuit, and frankly, "the worst" is sometimes a fairly accurate description of the person you are dealing with. However, you cannot forget that *both* parties to the lawsuit have been through the wringer. They have probably been just as tense and anxious for just as long as you have. You may be surprised to find out that both sides are glad it's over and settled, and both sides are ready to move forward with their lives.

This first meeting should be just the adults, so leave the kids at home. Everyone is likely to be at least a little anxious heading into this discussion. And frankly, you can't be sure how it will go. There is no reason to risk an uncomfortable scene for your children at this point. If this meeting goes well, there will be other opportunities to include the children. We will talk about that below.

Of course, you can extend the invitation and the other party may turn you down cold. They may be just as mad and argumentative as ever. If that is the case, do not force it. Again, this temperature check is an opportunity to lay down your arms and come together in an attempt to set a new tone for your co-parenting relationship. You cannot do that by dragging an unwilling party into it. If they say no, accept the answer and move on. Try to keep a good attitude and be aware of any assumptions you might be inclined to make about their behavior. Sure, they may not want to have this discussion because they don't want to be around you. They might even genuinely hate your guts. But it can be likely that they are simply too hurt or scared to meet with you now, especially when they are not officially *required* to do so. This is not only okay—it's also perfectly understandable. Just meet the person where they are emotionally and restart your co-parenting recovery from there.

Remember, the other party is still healing, just like you are. They may get to a place where they can share a meal and a cordial conversation with you—or they might not. You can't control that. You're responsible for *your* behavior, not theirs.

Strategies for Co-Parenting

Now that you've at least tried to demonstrate your intention to move forward peaceably with the new arrangement, it's time to discuss a few post-litigation co-parenting strategies. These are all good ideas for any co-parenting relationship at any time, but they're especially useful as you lay a new foundation for how you and your co-parent will interact after a lawsuit. The five strategies we'll cover here are:

1. Invite God into your co-parenting relationship.
2. Present a united front to the children.
3. Encourage the other parent and celebrate their wins.
4. Give the child space to make their own decisions about the other parent.
5. Take advantage of modern co-parenting tools.

Strategy 1: Invite God into Your Co-Parenting Relationship

Not to overstate the obvious, but the first step toward a healthy co-parenting relationship is to invite God into your relationship with your co-parent. This means, as crazy as it may sound to you in the middle of a lawsuit, you should be praying for your ex regularly. So often, we withhold prayer for people with whom we have a difficult relationship. Whether knowingly or not, we develop an inner belief that our ex is "the enemy," and that person doesn't *deserve* our prayers. That can lead to what we call an *inner vow* (something we will discuss more fully in a later chapter) that proclaims with our actions, *That person hurt me. If I pray for them, God might actually bless them, and I do not want that. So I will never pray for God to move in their life.*

This is not only a dangerous attitude for us as followers of Jesus; it's a self-defeating position that ultimately only brings more hardship and heartache upon ourselves and, worse, our children. Jesus calls us to pray for those who have hurt us. He tells us to "Love your enemies, do good to those who hate you, bless those who curse you, pray for those who abuse you" (Luke 6:27–28). Your ex-spouse, even under the worst conditions, should fall into at least one of those categories. If praying for the person dragging you through the legal system or the one you see as bitterly failing the children you share seems impossible, remember Paul's words in Romans:

Chapter 9 | 171

"Likewise the Spirit helps us in our weakness. For we do not know what to pray for as we ought, but the Spirit himself intercedes for us with groanings too deep for words" (Romans 8:26). That is, even when you cannot force yourself to articulate a healthy prayer for your ex, you can ask the Holy Spirit to step in and pray for your ex on your behalf. Ask God to work His will in that person's life and to bring grace and understanding into each of your hearts.

If this still sounds impossible, that's okay. We get it. God doesn't always call us to do what is *easy*. In fact, He rarely leads us down that road. Maybe you simply cannot pray for your ex by name today. If that's the case, ask God to work on your heart, bringing you into closer alignment and relationship with Him. Trust Him to work His will in every twist and turn, in every dark corner of your lawsuit, in your relationship with your ex, and in *both* parents that your children are counting on. Fall back on the wisdom of Proverbs, which promises, "Trust in the LORD with all your heart, and do not lean on your own understanding. In all your ways acknowledge him, and he will make straight your paths" (Proverbs 3:5–6).

STRATEGY 2: PRESENT A UNITED FRONT TO THE CHILDREN

Let's face it: children can be sneaky and manipulative—especially in a blended family situation. They can play off the fact that Mom and Dad don't live together and don't like having to talk to each other. This gives kids plenty of room to try convincing one parent of something, betting on the fact that the issue isn't worth making a phone call to the other parent.

Whenever possible, demonstrate to the children that the parents won't hesitate to talk to each other if there is a question or concern about the child. This can help prevent *triangulation*, which is when the child tries to play one parent off another. For example, let's say little Billy fails a test on Monday after spending the weekend at his father's house. Mom, upset about the test on Monday night, asks, "Did you study Sunday like you were supposed to?"

172 | Martindale & Brewer

Billy knows he didn't study nearly as much as he was supposed to. Instead, he spent all day Sunday fishing with his father. Assuming his parents don't *enjoy* talking, Billy weighs his options and takes a chance: "I told Dad I needed to study, but he told me I had to go fishing with him. He said it was important father-son time."

Mom has two options here. If she is unable or unwilling to communicate with her ex, she'll probably take precious Billy's word for it. She might even complain to him about how irresponsible his father is. In this case, Billy's bet paid off: he played his mother's hesitation about contacting his father against her, and he won.

Her second option, though not always ideal or frankly even possible, is to call Billy's bluff. She might say, "Really? That doesn't sound right. He knew you had an important test today. Let's just call him and see what he says." Then, Mom pulls out her phone, dials the number, and puts it on speaker as Billy shakes in his boots. He's busted, because even though his parents may not *like* talking, they are both *willing* to talk whenever it's in the best interest of their child.

How many more times do you think Billy would try this little tactic once he's been caught lying to one parent about what the other said or did?

When the child realizes Mom and Dad actually do work together on parenting, it removes the possibility of manipulation and triangulation. It also provides a sense of stability because the child knows both parents are still involved and active in raising him/her.

Obviously, it won't always be comfortable having a chat with your ex. Few people *want* that, especially in the aftermath of a long, costly, emotionally difficult custody modification case. But, and this is important, children need to know their parents are a united front. Billy needs to know that his mother loves him enough to have an awkward conversation with the person she least wants to talk to if she thinks it's necessary.

One way to communicate this clearly to your kids after the litigation is resolved is to reset the parent/child relationship together, ideally by sharing a meal together—the parents, the stepparents, and the children all sitting around a table together. This can be a powerful visual to your children. By having a somewhat uncomfortable dinner at a restaurant, you can demonstrate that Mom, Dad, and their spouses are all capable of sitting down together and having a nice time. You can use this time to let them know the litigation is over and explain the new agreement to the kids. Each parent can also get things off to a good start by showing support for the time the kids will spend with the other parent.

Except in cases of abuse (which should have been dealt with in the lawsuit), you should make sure the kids know you want them to have a good, positive, healthy relationship with both parents and be a part of both families. You will all attend sporting events, recitals, school functions, graduations, and weddings together as you move forward. All those future moments of awkwardness are probably weighing heavily on your children's minds. By sharing a meal and explaining the new custody agreement together, you are showing the children that you, your ex, and your spouses are still a parenting team and that you're all willing to work together for the good of the kids.

STRATEGY 3: ENCOURAGE THE OTHER PARENT AND CELEBRATE THEIR WINS

In many co-parenting situations, one parent (typically the father) only has the child on weekends, with maybe a midweek visit and a month or two in the summer. This does not give Dad many opportunities to parent. Dad's parenting muscles may not be as developed as Mom's, and he might therefore need some encouragement that he's doing a good job. In this situation, simply knowing Mom trusts the father to help the child study, get them to sports practice, and show up for recitals can go a long way toward shaping Dad into the father the child needs him to be.

This is especially true in a post-litigation setting when the outcome is far from what one party wanted. In most modification cases, *both* sides will feel like they didn't get exactly what they wanted. And in practically every case, you are going to have parties that are not 100 percent thrilled with the outcome. There is going to be some disappointment, and one party is likely to feel like they "lost" the case. Add to that all the time, financial, and emotional resources that were spent, and you are left with a lot of hard feelings and possibly a mountain of self-doubt. This can lead a disappointed and disillusioned parent to simply fade away into the background of the child's life. You may notice this as that parent calls less often, cancels their arranged weekends, stops showing up to activities, and so on. Because they cannot have the relationship they wanted with the child, they may choose not to pursue a relationship at all.

Having one parent check out physically and emotionally is obviously not in the best interest of the child. They'll be left wondering, "Why doesn't Dad want to spend time with me?" or "Why doesn't Mommy love me anymore?" These pervasive thoughts have a way of burying themselves deep in a person's psyche, taking root in the heart and mind and leaving the child with an overall sense of inadequacy or unlovability. As much as it is in your power, do not let this happen to your child! Children get so much of their personal self-worth from the love and attention they receive from their parents. If one parent isn't showing up, it is likely going to have a lasting negative effect on the child that can (and probably will) impact every relationship that child ever have.

So, if you are the parent who's guilty of emotionally and physically detaching from your child, you must get yourself together for the sake of your child. That means being on guard against any tendencies or behaviors that may be communicating a lack of interest or engagement in your parent-child relationship. It also means plugging back in as a parent and making sure your child knows you love them. Make your child a priority, even if it's not exactly under the terms you wanted in the court orders. If you are this parent, you owe it to your child to address these painful emotions and circumstances in a healthy way. The best way to do that is by seeking professional counseling and finding someone to guide you on a personalized healing journey after the trials of your litigation experience. Your child needs you and is worth the effort.

If you are the other parent who is noticing a gradual slide in your co-parent's engagement, challenge yourself to withhold criticism and think of things from their perspective. If they were seeking primary or 50/50 custody and did not get it, for example, they can easily feel deflated and undervalued as a parent. We've heard some fathers say things like, "If the judge doesn't give me at least 50/50 custody, I may not be a part of this kid's life at all." What they really might be saying is, "If the judge doesn't think I'm a good enough parent to get the arrangement I wanted, then maybe it's best for everyone if I just back off entirely."

If you find yourself and your family in this situation, be sure to encourage the fading parent. Make things easy for them to get or stay plugged in. Celebrate any parenting wins with them. Contact them to share good news. Proactively involve them in parental decision-making and work with your child to ensure a steady stream of communication with the missing parent. It may not seem fair (it probably isn't), you may not think your ex deserves your help (they probably don't), and it may be the last thing you want to do (it probably will be). But you are not doing this for the other parent; you're doing it for your child. Remember, the goal *after* litigation is the same as the goal *during* litigation: the best interest of the child. Abuse situations notwithstanding, having a strong relationship with both parents is almost always what's best for a child.

Strategy 4: Give the Child Space to Make Their Own Decisions About the Other Parent

We have discussed parent alienation several times already, but it's worth mentioning again in the post-litigation context. Oftentimes at the end of a lawsuit, when the persistent feeling of "parenting under a microscope" begins to fade, one parent will relax a little too much and grow careless with their words around their children. To put it bluntly, they start trash-talking the other parent to their kids. This is just as bad an idea in the Recovery phase as it was at any other point in the litigation process. When you speak ill of the other parent to or in front of your children, you are actively harming them. We can't state it any clearer than that. *You are hurting your kids and jeopardizing your own relationship with your children.*

How so?

When we speak ill of the other parent, we are trying to influence the child's attitude about and relationship with that parent. Rather than giving the child the opportunity to form their own opinions of who that parent is, how that parent behaves, and how well that parent functions as a mom or dad, we're putting ourselves in the middle of that relationship. We're telling the child what *we* think of the other parent—sometimes with an expectation (spoken or unspoken) that the child should take *our* side *against* the other parent. This has the potential to blow up in our faces, sending the child running to the other parent and away from us.

For example, you might be in a situation in which your child wanted to go live with the other parent, but that is not where things landed. The child can take out their anger and frustration on you, and it can be tempting to argue back to them all the reasons why it would be a terrible idea for them to live with the other parent. In this situation, the child is not able to accept those reasons, no matter how sound they may be. The child is upset about not getting the change they wanted, and that is a valid emotional response.

Don't try to "make" them think, feel, or believe *anything* about the situation. Just love them well, provide a safe home, and pray for them to accept the court orders.

Or maybe your ex acted horribly toward you throughout the litigation, throwing around wild accusations and saying terrible things about you. Obviously, that hurts. Moreover, it is infuriating. In those situations, it becomes easy to convince ourselves that we're "protecting" our kids by "telling them the truth" about the other parent. Again, this is a recipe for disaster. When we do this, we are forcing the child to make an impossible choice. The message comes across loud and clear: "You can have a relationship with *them*, or you can have a relationship with *me*. You can't have both." And that's a scenario in which everyone loses.

So do not go into detail about everything that happened during the litigation in an attempt to make yourself look good or the other parent look bad. Keep your conversation with your child about the other parent positive and focused on your commitment to operate as a parenting team. In time, most children come to realize on their own the benefit of how the orders worked out.

If there is a bad or unhealthy parent in the mix, the child will usually come to realize the truth in time on their own. It is always best if the child figures this out rather than having the opinion of the other parent influenced by you. That way, if there is a bad parent involved, the child will still have you. However, if you've alienated the child from you by trying to convince your child of how bad the other parent is, your child is left with bad relationships with both parents, and that's a lose-lose situation.

STRATEGY 5: TAKE ADVANTAGE OF MODERN CO-PARENTING TOOLS

We've spent a lot of time talking about an "ideal" co-parenting situation with two parents who are at least able to communicate, even though they may not want to. Sadly, that's not always the case coming out of a hard-fought lawsuit. In the aftermath of litigation, talking to your ex is probably near the top of your "Don't Wanna Do It" list. Trying to function as a parenting team for your children and yet desperately never wanting to talk each other again can be tricky.

The number-one ground rule for a good co-parenting relationship post-litigation is to keep the focus on the children. However, you may be dealing with a person you do not trust very much, and they probably feel the same about you. You will likely never be close friends with your co-parent and his/her spouse, but that's okay. You don't have to be friends. You just have to be good co-parents for your children.

A great way to work together and exchange safe, reliable communication in both good times and bad is to use modern family co-parenting apps and online tools. This has been a game-changer over the past decade, because these tools and services have simplified what was once perhaps the most difficult and challenging aspect of co-parenting: simple communication. These tools are so useful that they are now commonly included in the final orders a family receives through a custody modification case in many states.

Many Texas family courts, for example, including ones in our jurisdiction, include the Our Family Wizard app and service (www.ourfamilywizard.com) in the final orders. In fact, this service was included in Scott and Vanessa's modification orders a few years ago. Another option that's becoming common is the Family Core service (www.thefamilycore.com). The great thing about these and other co-parenting tools is that anyone can sign up for them. They don't *have* to be included in your family orders (although that's the best option to ensure both parties actually *use* it). So, if your orders do not instruct the parties to use one of these tools, you can discuss options with your co-parent and incorporate these tools to simplify and consolidate your communication, calendars, and more.

Most of these tools—whether you choose Our Family Wizard, Family Core, or another option—offer similar features. Typically, this includes:

- **Communication:** In-app text messaging and email. Many co-parents *only* communicate through the app. This takes the pressure off feeling like you must phone your ex when you need to share information.
- **Calendar:** Each parent, stepparent, and child can access a shared calendar to take the ambiguity out of sporting events, recitals, school functions, and child drop-off and pickup.
- **Expense Tracking:** You can share receipts through the app for reimbursement from the other parent, discuss major expenses for the child, etc.
- **Health and Safety:** The app provides a central repository for children's health records.
- **Activity Journal:** It's easy to keep a record of children's coming and going, if one parent was late picking up or dropping off, when and how a parent violated the terms of the court order, and so on.
- **Documentation:** Provides a paper trail of all communication, expenses, and scheduling issues.
- **Court Access:** When ordered by the court, the attorneys and other agents of the court can access the records when there is a question about compliance or enforcement.

Again, the features differ among the different services, but this gives you a rough idea of what to expect if you start looking at different options. Again, though, the best option is to have this added to your court papers. Ask your attorney before the papers are finalized if such a tool is standard in your area. If not, see if you can add it to your final order as a requirement.

A Season of Growth

If your boss gave you an intense, all-encompassing, month-long performance evaluation at your job, during which your entire professional life and every job-related task you did was put under a microscope and heavily scrutinized by a team of experts, you would probably take their recommendations very seriously. You would seek to improve the areas they saw as weaknesses, and you would build on areas they saw as strengths. You would dig into the issues they raised and research the resources they recommended to you as potential aids in your work. You would recognize that these professionals had a vested interest in making you the very best employee you could possibly be, and you'd want to meet that expectation. After all, your job, your career, your very livelihood would depend on it.

A custody litigation suit is a lot like a high-pressure, in-depth performance review. However, instead of grading your professional performance, a team of experts is judging your aptitude as a parent and co-parent. In addition to lawyers and judges, you might have had parent facilitators, parent coordinators, mediators, social workers, psychologists, and counselors all rummaging through every nook and cranny of your parenting life. They no doubt found every strength and weakness, every win and failure, and brought them out into the light of day for intense examination. It is an excruciating process, but now, it's finally over.

So what are you going to take away from this (hopefully) once-in-a-lifetime experience?

A natural response to a tough custody fight is to get bitter and defensive: "I can't believe what they said about me! Who do they think they are? What do they know about my situation?"

A better response is to use their findings to take an honest, critical look at yourself: "I'm embarrassed about those old text messages they read in court. I was mortified when the opposing lawyer asked me to explain the nasty voicemail I left for my ex that they played out loud for everyone to hear. That's not who I want to be as a person or as a parent. I can be better than that."

By learning from those painful lessons and incorporating what you've learned into your new life as a parent and co-parent, you can extract value and meaning from your otherwise awful litigation journey. You'll turn the worst thing that ever happened to you into a springboard that launches you into becoming the best possible version of yourself.

Prolonged family court litigation isn't cheap. It comes with substantial emotional and financial cost, and it eats up months of your life. It is one of the most expensive experiences of your life. It would be a shame if you spent all that time, money, and emotional energy and didn't bother to apply any of what you learned to improve your life.

Coming out of your litigation, you can go right back to who you've always been, right back to parenting the same way, right back to working with (or not working with) your co-parent just as you always have. Or you can be better. A better parent. A better co-parent. A better spouse. A better *you*.

You paid a lot to get here—wherever "here" is for you now.

Don't waste the education you just bought. Use it to transform your life for good.

Chapter 10

A BATTLE WORTH FIGHTING

Scott

My family's tour of duty through the battleground of litigation ended several years ago. Our son, Michael, was 12 when his father filed the lawsuit that kicked things off. As I sit here writing this, he's heading into his senior year of high school. We are talking about colleges and which ones he wants to tour this year. He'll be 18 in just a few months, and that will conclude the custody orders we fought so hard to obtain. He'll be an adult—legally, anyway. (Were any of us *really* "adults" at 18?) At that point, he'll be free to choose what kind of relationship he wants with his dad and with us. As far as the court is concerned, he'll be free to live wherever he wants and spend as much (or as little) time as he wants with any of us.

Putting the litigation season in perspective, we spent about 13 months and tens of thousands of dollars fighting tooth and nail. We lived in a persistent state of fear and stress. Our focus was constantly being pulled away from our three youngest boys, who were four years old and younger at the time. We were not able to give each of them the time and attention they deserved. The entire Martindale family—all six of us—paid a steep price for that court battle. And for what? Only five years' worth of time with Michael? Was it worth it?

If you're reading this book, you already know the answer to that question.

We've seen miracles happen in our family and specifically in Michael's life over the past few years. We've watched him grow into a mature, confident young man who loves his family and is able to *receive* love from us. We've seen him own his role as "big brother" to his three much-younger siblings, who all adore Michael. We've seen him grow in his walk with the Lord, getting baptized just a few months after the litigation ended—with both sets of parents watching from their seats side by side. We've seen him manage the ups and downs of living in two households. We've seen him discover on his own how misguided some of his assumptions were about us, about his father, and about our court battle. He's *grown up* over the last several years, and we couldn't be prouder of the young man he is and the man he is becoming.

Would Michael be who and what he is today if we hadn't fought so hard for what we believed was best for him?

No.

We had to go through the entire process outlined in this book to land on an agreement that was something we could live with but, more importantly, something that was in the best interest of our son.

Our lengthy custody litigation bought us five years or so with our son, but those have been probably the most important, life-shaping years of his life. He didn't realize it at the time and frankly, he doesn't fully realize it even now, but those years laid the foundation for who he is today and who he will be ten, twenty, and fifty years from now.

The battle we've fought—the battle *you're* fighting now—is hard, long, stressful, and expensive. But it is the most important fight of your life.

No matter how bad things have been, how bad things are right now as you read this, or how bad they get tomorrow, don't lose sight of that fact.

Our children are worth fighting for.

Cut Corners, Not Phases

The process we have unpacked in this book is extensive and thorough. This is the full-court press, all-in, do-what-it-takes plan of attack. This means it is also expensive. What we have laid out here takes enormous amounts of time and money. Depending on your budget, you may need to cut some corners here and there. We understand that, but always keep the big picture in mind to ensure you are not cutting something that could come back to bite you later. We've tried to be reasonable in this book about indicating things that are *must-haves* and things that are *nice-to-haves*. Don't skimp on the *must-haves*.

Most importantly, even if you must pick and choose which areas to focus on and which battles to fight, do not leave out an entire phase of the litigation journey we've unpacked here. The phases of litigation that we've discussed throughout this book represent a thorough, complete journey through the whole process. If you go through litigation and leave out any phase, specifically Preparation or Recovery (since you can't exactly skip the Execution phase), you are doing yourself and your family a disservice. It not only puts the outcome of your litigation in jeopardy, but it also puts the future health and happiness of your whole blended family in jeopardy.

Dennis

Remember that family law cases involving children are different from any other kind of lawsuit in one major way: When the case is over, the two parties are not going their separate ways. They are stuck together for at least many years, and to a lesser degree will be in each other's orbit for life.

If you have a business-related lawsuit or a personal injury lawsuit from a car wreck, it takes place at one point in history. These events and people eat up a lot of time and energy, but you know there will be a day when they are gone forever. Once the case is resolved, the parties part ways.

But in family law cases where there are minor children, the two parties are intertwined forever. Obviously, there is a tight connection until the children turn eighteen, but even then, both parties will remain a part of each other's world in some capacity. You will still share weddings, grandchildren, and other key family events for the rest of your life. And while your children are still young, you are all responsible for the development and welfare of these kids. Again, it is not about what's comfortable. It is about what is best for your child, what is going to prepare them best for life, what will prepare them emotionally for their own future relationships, and so on. So, while the litigation takes place at one point in time, the relationships—good or bad—stay for the long haul. Use this *forever* mentality to give you the extra incentive you need to work the whole process—Preparation *and* Execution *and* Recovery. Hopefully, by going the extra mile, you'll get through this litigation and still have a healthy, manageable relationship with your co-parents, with your kids, and with your spouse.

Support For Your Blended Family

Obviously, the end of litigation doesn't signal the end of your relationship with your co-parents. Your new final orders only represent the close of one chapter and the start of another. The papers will lay the ground rules and provide new guardrails for your relationship, but they aren't going to tell you how to develop into a healthy blended family. For that, you need some resources that your attorney and the family court system don't supply. These are resources that will help you continue to develop as a husband, wife, mother, father, stepparent, ex-spouse, and co-parent.

Think of it like surgery. When your body has a life-and-death crisis, you need nurses, paramedics, a surgeon, an operating room, and maybe a short hospital stay. Afterward, your doctor might hand you over to a physical therapist who will introduce you to a program of specific exercises tailor-made to help your body recover over the long haul. What does that have to do with your family court case? The lawsuit was the life-and-death crisis. But instead of doctors, nurses, and hospitals, you got judges, lawyers, and courtrooms. This team of experts led you through the "surgery" (your litigation) but they aren't the ones who will stick with you long-term and help you develop the new "muscles" you need to heal as a blended family. For that, you need specific resources, just like you need physical therapy after surgery.

Scott

Sadly, this is a huge need met by too few resources for too long. There have not been sufficient resources to meet the needs of all the single parent and blended family households out there. That is why Vanessa and I started our ministry, Blended Kingdom Families (BKF). We each grew up in blended families. When we married, we started a blended family of our own. We looked for support resources for a long time—books, workshops, classes at church, etc.—but kept coming up dry. There just were not many options for families like ours who were looking for education, support, and community specifically designed for blended families. So, after a season of prayer and searching, God led us to launch BKF and do whatever we could to fill the void ourselves.

As we outline in our mission statement, BKF exists to break the generational cycle of divorce, equip marriages, and unite blended families with the truth of God's Word. Our vision is to provide every blended family with a local church and group to receive equipping and support both spiritually and physically. It's a big goal, but we feel called to this work and are amazed at what God has done in, through, and for BKF over these past several years.

If you need support for your blended family (if you're going through or coming out of litigation, you definitely do), then please visit us online at blendedkingdomfamilies.com. You can also pick up our book, *Blended and Redeemed: The Go-To Field Guide for the Modern Stepfamily*, which covers all the key areas of blended family living, including support for your marriage, raising your children, working with (or simply *dealing* with) your ex, blending two sets of kids into a single bunch of siblings, and more.

God Still Has Room To Work

Now, as we wrap things up, we want to close this book with one important point. This point is universally true no matter how smooth or bumpy your litigation journey has been. This is something that is true whether you and your ex settled the matter out of court on Day One or if one of you dragged the other through a year-long, hard-fought, crazy-expensive mudslinging escapade in the halls of the county court. No matter what's happened up to this point, no matter who you think "won" and "lost," and no matter what you had to sacrifice to take the exit ramp off the family court highway, please remember this:

You and your co-parent are bound by the new court orders you've received.

But God is not.

Just because you have a new set of final orders, that doesn't mean God can't or won't work in, through, around, and over your new court papers. The orders are final in the eyes of the court, but God can still work miracles.

For example, after litigating your case, you and your ex may end up with a 50/50 custody split. That may not even be close to what you wanted, but it's where you landed, and you are obligated to honor the arrangement. Now, you may feel stuck in the finality of the orders, but God may just be getting started. He can still do amazing things—miraculous things—in your situation. The new arrangement may end up being exactly what everyone needed. Maybe your ex, whom you didn't trust at the start, will step up as a parent now that they are *actively parenting* more than ever. Who benefits most from a better, more engaged parent? Your child! In this situation, your ex experiences a radical transformation, and your child experiences a great relationship with both parents. That's a huge blessing, but it may not be one you can see in the immediate aftermath of the litigation.

Or you may finally land on that 50/50 arrangement after a long, hard fight, only to have your ex suddenly decide to move halfway across the country and give up their new split-custody arrangement six months later. Problem solved! Of course, you'll still deal with a huge amount of frustration over this outcome. It'd be fair to say, "You mean we went through a year of hell and spent tens of thousands of dollars only to end up right back where we started?" Yep. Totally possible. It's not up to you. We're not saying the outcome will make sense. We're only saying you have no idea what God might do next week, next month, or next year. All we can do is accept the resolution, thank God for still working miracles, and trust that He has a purpose in all of this.

We've seen both of these surprising outcomes and more in the many blended families we've worked with over the years. We've seen mostly absent, nightmarishly bad parents grow up and become the fathers or mothers their child needed. We've seen hateful, vile parents sue their ex for sport and end up losing all parental rights in the process. We've seen litigation literally save children's lives by uncovering abuse and other dangerous situations that no one knew about until the court started poking around. We've seen healthy, loving blended families heal from the wounds of litigation and come out surprisingly *stronger* and *happier* than ever. We've seen people come running to God (or *back* to God)—literally changing the trajectory of their lives from now and into eternity—because of the horrible fear, anxiety, stress, and emotional turmoil of their custody case. We've seen it all. Well, almost all.

The one thing we haven't seen, the one thing *none* of us have seen, is what surprising, out-of-nowhere blessings God will bring out of *your* experience. God can turn this terrifying mine field you've been tiptoeing through into a field of green grass and sunflowers. As the apostle Paul proclaims, "And we know that in all things God works for the good of those who love him, who have been called according to his purpose" (Romans 8:28 NIV). You might think, *All things? I'm not sure how God can use any of this mess for our good.* Perhaps you cannot see it now, but God is in the business of turning trash into eternal treasure!

About seven hundred years before Jesus' earthly ministry, the prophet Isaiah told us exactly what Jesus' mission would be:

> The Spirit of the Sovereign LORD is on me,
> because the LORD has anointed me
> to proclaim good news to the poor.
> He has sent me to bind up the brokenhearted,
> to proclaim freedom for the captives
> and release from darkness for the prisoners,
> to proclaim the year of the LORD's favor
> and the day of vengeance of our God,
> to comfort all who mourn,
> and provide for those who grieve in Zion—
> to bestow on them a crown of beauty
> instead of ashes,
> the oil of joy
> instead of mourning,
> and a garment of praise
> instead of a spirit of despair (Isaiah 61:1–3 NIV).

He brings comfort to the mourning. He takes our dirty ashes and gives us a crown of beauty. He replaces our mourning with joy and our despair with praise.

God is our Redeemer. That means He is also redeeming our horrible, no-good, lousy, stinking, family court litigation battle. There are certainly bad days—a *lot* of bad days. We won't deny that, and we won't try to sugarcoat your misery by saying something trite. But we know from experience gained by serving in the trenches with hundreds of blended families just like yours that what you're going through right now isn't the whole story.

It isn't even the *end* of the story.

It's just a chapter.

And God's still writing the next one.

ACKNOWLEDGMENTS

Writing a book like this is never a one- or two-man show. To the many wonderful people who helped us get this book out of our heads and into the hands of the blended families who need it, we thank you.

Together, we would like to especially express our gratitude to our Lord and Savior, Jesus Christ, who freely offers not only the gift of salvation but also the promise of complete redemption and restoration. May this book guide suffering families into His loving hands.

Scott

To my incredible wife, Vanessa: You are my partner, my best friend, and the love of my life. Thank you for your unwavering love and support through all of life's ups and downs. I am beyond blessed to be your husband.

To my sons, Michael, Shay, Gray, and Kace: You bring me so much joy. Michael, watching you grow into a godly young man is one of the great privileges of my life. Shay, Gray, and Kace, your enthusiasm and zest for life never fail to make me smile. I'm so proud to be your dad.

To the teams at Blended Kingdom Families and Sevn Therapy: Your passion for strengthening families is inspiring. Your work matters, and I'm so glad you've chosen to do that work with us. And to Rachel, my wonderful assistant: I don't know what I'd do without you keeping everything running smoothly.

To Brent and Stephanie Evans and the incredible team at XO Marriage: Your friendship and shared mission mean the world to me. Your constant drive to strengthen marriages and families is truly amazing to experience.

To Allen, my editor: I can't wait to see what books we dream up together next.

To the Blended Kingdom Families community: Your stories, prayers, and support make our work possible. My heart is full of gratitude.

Dennis

Special thanks to Sueda, my "better-half," to whom I thankfully pleaded my case to marry me 43 years ago! And to my daughters, Alexandra and Mackenzie; sons-in-law, Andrew and Mauricio; and grandkids, Augustine (Gus), Arik, Rowen, Elena, and Luca, who constantly remind Sueda and me of the beauty of family.

To Fellowship Church, our amazing church that continues to impact my life week after week in countless ways; and my "Bro," Ed Young, his amazing wife, Lisa, and the unparalleled staff and volunteers that Ed leads across the campuses of Fellowship Church.

To my Dad, who lived his life to the fullest, for giving me amazing cases to work on at the beginning of my career, for getting me into the courtroom early and often, for showing me the ropes, and for demonstrating what can happen when you represent your clients zealously, tirelessly, and professionally.

To all the incredible dedicated family law attorneys, family court judges, parent facilitators, coordinators, counselors, and evaluators who are neck-deep in custody litigation week in and week out. Thank you for fighting for parents' rights, for protecting children, and for working skillfully and relentlessly toward the best outcome for each and every child impacted by the work you do.

Last but not least, thank you to my family law clients who chose to hire me, trusted me to be their attorney and counselor, and allowed me to lead them through the gauntlet during some of the most trying times of their lives. I think about you often.

BLENDED & REDEEMED

THE GO-TO FIELD GUIDE FOR THE MODERN STEPFAMILY
STUDY GUIDE

Designed for Individuals, Couples, and Small Groups/Classes

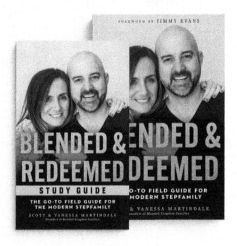

Scott and Vanessa take couples and groups through each chapter of the book for a deep dive into the topics of blended families. Each chapter of the study guide coincides with the chapter of the same number in the book. We highly recommend reading both the book and the study guide in order to gain the most understanding.

BLENDEDANDREDEEMED.COM

Marriage Help

We understand that when your marriage is struggling, you need help in a timely manner. XO Marriage is here to support you and stand alongside you in the fight for your marriage. We offer two distinct services:

Coaching on Call
Offered at multiple lengths, these sessions are designed for couples or individuals who are in crisis and need immediate help. Specializing in marital crisis intervention, our team is available to meet you in your time of need to listen with compassion and understanding, provide wise objective counsel, and help you navigate the best plan of action to start the healing process.

Marriage Mediation
Our full day private one-on-one marriage mediation is designed for couples who are struggling with multiple issues and/or feeling hopeless about the future of their marriage. This intensive approach allows couples the extended time needed to fully process their primary issues without the interruption of time or hassle of scheduling multiple weekly sessions.

To learn more, visit **xomarriage.com/help**.

www.ingramcontent.com/pod-product-compliance
Lightning Source LLC
Jackson TN
JSHW011948131224
75386JS00042B/1608